UNLIKELY ICON

*The Art, Culture, and Philosophy of Forest
Hills Cemetery, Boston: A Nineteenth
Century Symbol of American Values*

Diane Elizabeth Kelleher

authorHOUSE®

AuthorHouse™
1663 Liberty Drive, Suite 200
Bloomington, IN 47403
www.authorhouse.com
Phone: 1-800-839-8640

First published by AuthorHouse 4/24/2008
ISBN: 978-1-4343-6967-3 (sc)

Library of Congress Control Number: 2008901207

Printed in the United States of America
Bloomington, Indiana

This book is printed on acid-free paper.

For my mother, Hildur Englund Kelleher.

ACKNOWLEDGEMENTS

What's so interesting about a cemetery? What's so interesting about Forest Hills Cemetery? The search for answers to these questions prompted the research and writing of this book. Positioned within the context of historical perspective, this unusual topic of inquiry provides *a propos* insights into the ideological life of our Nation's values, presented within the format of unexpectedly informative, interesting reading. Written for both historians and the casual reader, the intent of this work has been twofold: first, to present the result of research endeavors, information hopefully useful and welcomed by others similarly intrigued by this topic; and secondly, for the leisure-time reader, to offer a casual text, though admittedly one focused on a topic rarely embraced in such a manner.

As we begin our journey in 1846, when the cemetery was barren farmland, cataloging its transformation throughout the ensuing decades up to the year 1900, in addition to considering its historical development, we will explore the larger context from which Forest Hills Cemetery emerged; that is, what we can learn from such places, what rural cemeteries reflected about the art and society from which they arose.

Throughout the process of ferreting out information, generous accessibility and gracious cooperation was offered by the following sources, and proved to be especially helpful: the general, research, rare books, and municipal records departments of the Boston Public Library; Boston University's Graduate School of Arts and Sciences Library; and, of course, various land records and minutes of the annual reports maintained in the library at Forest Hills Cemetery. Hopefully, the results of this work's methodology will provide valuable facts and insights for the general reader, as well as the more specialized historian. Contained herein, for example, are the references to accomplishments of landscape architects Emerson and Fehmer, Van Brundt and Howe, Alexander Esty, which would be of interest to architectural historians. Consistently, my intent has been to explain the existence, not only of a particular cemetery, but to reveal the cultural context and specific information of which the cemetery is merely an exemplary - unlikely icon. Hopefully, the following text, appendixes and bibliography will stimulate further interest, research and writing in this curious area of life and death.

DEK
Shrewsbury, Massachusetts, 1981.

INTRODUCTION

Above the traffic of the Jamaicaway, far removed from the harried sounds of twentieth century Boston, tiny wrens and sparrows still alight amidst the boughs of evergreens and elms with much the same curiosity, the same certainty of safety and solitude, as have what by now must be several generations of their predecessors. Indeed, during their short lifetimes, untallied flocks of birds, enchanting creatures of the natural world, have taken refuge in Forest Hills Cemetery as a haven of peace, their sanctuary of repose, a welcome topographical foil juxtaposed against a harsh, industrial world; and this, in much the same spirit as the souls of our ancestors. He who has stood in the Field of Manoah knows: Dawn creeps in, quiet in demeanor here, making it all the more difficult and intriguing to imagine, amidst the solitude of today, the sights and sounds and activities of yesteryear's beasts of burden, crews of common workmen, politicians, visionaries, intellectuals, architects and horticulturists, all working in unison and perhaps occasionally dissension and disharmony, to create landscape architectural history, nearly 150 years ago.

While it is true that in the twentieth century, cemeteries have become predominantly and exclusively, eternal homes, resting places for the deceased, that is, homes for souls; in the nineteenth, the identity of cemeteries were ambiguously this, as well as perpetual resting places, homes, for ideas. Derived from the principles of an era preceding their own as served them well, the validity of which remains notably unchanged to this day, cemeteries also iconized contemporary trends. In the nineteenth century, Bostonians perceived their own access to local cemeteries in a manner far different, less fearful, less specifically constrained, than their twentieth century counterparts, in large measure because cemetery innovations of the nineteenth century were part and parcel of the broader landscape architectural movement, stimulated by ideas imported mainly from England, emerging as both fashionable and functional, and very much in vogue.

Designed to engage the living, cemeteries came to be conceived, executed, and perceived as rural parks. This meant that cemeteries were in fact: horticultural showcases, engineering experiments, the physical embodiments of ideas drawn from social philosophy and politics, art historical archetypes born of historical precedent and presented for emulation, botanical gardens, outdoor statuary and pavilion museums, the playground for political maneuverings of Boston politicians, and, surprisingly, social gathering places from the Civil War through the Victorian era.

Here and now, under this cloudless sky of bluebird hue, on this crisp October morning alongside verdantly hilly lawns sprinkled lightly with orange, red, and amber, in this season so special to New Englanders; we will share our twentieth century stroll through the various divisions and dimensions of this outdoor masterpiece of nineteenth century landscape architecture with our companions overhead: birds in flight from pavilion to patio, pine tree to plot, pond to pastureland. Indeed, our companions are gentle, sharp-eyed, chattering, diminutive creatures, capable of seeing all, knowing all, as the undaunted witnesses of seasons of progress and change. They are the annual heralds of Spring, who like the cemetery workmen of an earlier time, abandon their stations in Winter intent upon returning with the first warmth of Spring to check old familiar places, and begin their work anew. Flying high above us, they and their winged ancestors have conveniently enjoyed the unique vantage point of aerial perspective, a bird's eye view that afforded an all encompassing glimpse from which to scrutinize any alteration in the landscape, note any changes and accomplishments, witness the outcomes of decisions made in the privacy of the political boardroom, accompany workmen on daily tasks, see the sadness, relief, ambiguity of burials, the pleasure of loving promenadeurs and blossomings of new botanical life; only to then, so easily and capriciously dart off, traversing our territory and that of our neighbors, to compare observations and progress occurring in a nearby cemetery.

Imagine for a moment if we could translate and catalogue the dialectical comments of these high flying creatures which charm us as cemetery visitors: these birds could then provide us with tales spanning years of observation, could easily recount what they have seen and what we will come to know through research, photography, and analysis, as we traverse the very same routes as have our feathery hosts. Silent witnesses were their ancestors not only to all associated emotions, but to a more God fearing, God revering time, to changing seasons of life, to the home of death, in an era wherein death was less perceived like the coldest snowflake of winter, a chill ending, but like the joyously colored leaves of fall revered in hushed and whispering tones as the timely, Heavenly, God-fearing devout's timely reward to a well-lived life.

Peaceful, solitary and beautiful are adjectives which aptly describe Forest Hills Cemetery, yesterday and today. As an oasis of botanical and horticultural gentility, indeed comparatively more striking by virtue of both its proximity to the urbanity of Boston and the aesthetic sublimity of its sister cemetery nestled in nearby Cambridge; Forest Hills Cemetery evolved under the guidance of landscape architect Henry Dearborn, and reflected multi-faceted cultural concerns raised at a fervent time in American history. Understandably, Forest Hills Cemetery emerged as a straight-forward response to questions of public health and safety centered upon the unhealthy burial practices and overcrowded conditions of neighboring cemeteries. Unexpectedly, as we delve more deeply behind its surface appearances into its philosophical, cultural, and art historical causes, context and precedents; we are surprised by the number and extent of direct and indirect influences absorbed from so many ideational sources and individual groups, both here and abroad, which have come to bear upon its creation.

On an operational and architectural level, Henry S. Dearborn; his Scottish Superintendent, Mr. Brims; Cambridge colleague, Jacob Bigelow, a fellow collaborator associated with Mount Auburn Cemetery; the Boston architectural firm of Pierce, Fenner, and Smith; and landowners, Seaverns and Warren; are but a few of the names ready to assume commonplace familiarity as we explore their impact. Played out within the context of daily roles and responsibilities, we will learn how the web of their activities directly shaped the physical appearance of Forest Hills Cemetery.

Culturally, equally important, were the ideas of the era - its *zeitgeist*. Conceptually, the most significant contributors, destined to define the cultural milieu, that is, the pervasive ideational context from which Forest Hills Cemetery emerged and the underlying abstractions which advance its theory and clarify our understanding of the cemetery's meaning within its own era are the Rural Cemetery Movement, itself a product of a larger phenomenon, the Beautification Drives of the nineteenth century, and their various associated factors and factions. Categorized fourfold, these groups perpetuated ideas transmitted by: Americans traveling in Europe; Transcendentalists; Post-Transcendentalist Art Publicists, and America's Conservatives, whose emphasis on civic values actually look back toward Platonic and Neo-Platonic Republicanism.

The parameters of American history have consistently enclosed particular traditional values: capitalism, civic pride, Anglo-Saxon American competition; the desire to escape from industrialism to retreat to an agrarian refuge; and an established spiritual reverence, ready to join forces with a new religion: the Cult of Nature: all of which found points of reference within the various factions of the nineteenth century Beautification

Movement. Yet, there were broader issues: a sort of immanent manifest destiny continuously affecting the American psyche, which applauded greater and greater acquisition of the beloved American gemstone: Land; the popularity, especially in New England alcoves, of Transcendentalist philosophy and its reverence and imbuement and intertwining of nature, spiritualism, and man (ontology) not entirely unlike the gentler expression of Northern Romanticism in Europe; and a basic reassessment and redefinition of the relationships between such seemingly stalwartly concepts as Man and Nature, Art and Society, God and Cosmology. Nineteenth century America was, after all, the age of Empiricism and Metaphysics, but most importantly, of American Ontology - a force which pervaded Transcendentalist, Republicans, Naturalists, and other painters, poets, patrons, and formulators of thought. Truthfully, the mere fact that the objectification of these issues, concerns, and values extended to such apparently unlikely ends as a cemetery, is evidence of the extent to which these philosophies impacted, and these values merged with American thought and society. The cemetery itself is as the individual grave, both end and new beginning and timeless symbol.

In the more specialized area of aesthetic precedent and art historical archetypes, European notions exemplified abroad in the work of English landscape architects: John Nash, the creator of London's Regence Park, and Sir Henry Repton, thankfully found their way from European to American soil through writings of Andrew Jackson Downing. In a general way, our exploration of the values of aesthetician, Edmund Burke, in conjunction, with a contrasting analysis of Mount Auburn Cemetery in Cambridge, Massachusetts, sheds light on our understanding of Forest Hills' relative position with respect to issues of sublimity and beauty - an issue of critical aesthetic significance to this particular century of their creation.

Of course, in October, the beautiful is still readily apparent to us as the cemetery reveals itself: its handpicked arboreal enhancements, its statuary, and the splendor of its naturalistic combinations of verdant lawns, ornithological stations, the splendor of its hand-dug pond reflecting the blue vault of Heaven as it encloses rows of magnificent, old pines stretching upward as if to greet the blue vault of Heaven. We will learn also of the botanical exotica imported from the best European catalogues of the day, which half a century after Paul Revere's ride through New England, still grace the same carriage roads. Not until the Victorian era would we again encounter such an interest in Nature, such an insatiable love affair with these botanical marvels from life and lexicons, as emerge from the reflections of eyes tilted toward beautification in honor of hands which once planted and caressed resplendent examples, in deep appreciation and delight in these delicate, colorful creations we and our Boston ancestors call simply, flowers.

Standing amidst this verdant beauty, as we are surrendered to an otherworldly sense of respite, it is easy to reflect and query a moment, about how vastly different were the country's regional, funerary customs. Indeed, Panter's Gothic Gateway, Dearborn's Egyptian gate, the pre-Civil War statuary, and the imported exotica found at Forest Hills; and the breath-taking topographical drama of her sister cemetery, Mount Auburn, stand in cosmopolitan splendor, when contrasted with the more austere, practical, unembellished plots of the agrarian locales of the Shakers, or Yankee and mid-Western farmers. Here again, basic philosophy steps forward - the philosophy of a era, the philology of Forest Hills' designer, and those of its predecessor.

TABLE OF CONTENTS

The Beautification Movement...Ambiguous Influences of European Travel...Transcendentalism..Post-Transcendentalist Art Publicists...Conservatives...Other Perspectives/ Other Writers.

The Indirect Influence of Sir Henry Repton. Mount Auburn and Forest Hills Cemeteries: Two American Prototypes, Similarities and Differences.

Decades of Decisions: The Eighteen - Forties, Fifties, Sixties, Seventies, Eighties and Nineties.

SECTION I:

FOREST HILLS CEMETERY: THE CULTURAL AND PHILOSOPHICAL CONTEXT

SECTION I

FOREST HILLS CEMETERY:
THE CULTURAL AND PHILOSOPHICAL CONTEXT

An oasis of gentility, all the more striking for its urban location, Forest Hills Cemetery is, today, located in Jamaica Plain, near Boston, Massachusetts; and currently consists of 260 acres of knolls, woods, plateaus, and level pastureland, all devoted to family and single burial lots, meticulously maintained under a system of perpetual care. The grounds are bounded on the northeast by Morton Street, the east by Canterbury Street, and the south by Walk Hill Street. This rural cemetery is owned by the proprietors and managed by a seven member Board of Trustees which oversees the management of this non-sectarian cemetery. Perusal of a contemporary marketing brochure would inform of this much; but we are interested to know more than merely the descriptive, physical facts. We want to know about art and society and thought in America as it is revealed to us through this icon called Forest Hills Cemetery.

Forest Hills Cemetery emerged from the larger Rural Cemetery Movement which had taken root in the 1830s and had previously given rise to Mount Auburn Cemetery in Cambridge, Massachusetts

(1831), Greenwood in Brooklyn (1838), Greenmount in Baltimore, Laurel Hill in Philadelphia (1836), and Mount Hope in Rochester, to mention but a few. (1)

The Rural Cemetery Movement was itself an extension of the larger, more profound drives immanent in American culture; an extension of what author, Neil Harris, in his The Artist in American Society: The Formative Years, 1790-1860, calls the Beautification Drives of the nineteenth century, which were associated with the creation of parks and the erection of monuments, and which anticipated and resurfaced during our own century, in the beautification drives of the Johnson presidency, spear-headed by First Lady, Lady Bird Johnson. Initially, the creation of rural cemeteries was a reformist gesture made by a variety of groups for a variety of reasons. What these groups shared was an "enthusiasm for social control, restraint of passions and national unanimity," (2) wherein we recognize the emergence of Platonic and Neo-Platonic virtues of Republicanism: nobility, restraint and constraint, cognition of higher goals wedded to an aesthetic whose primacy extolled a search for God and Beauty.

Many of the concerns, goals and attributes which shaped the Beautification Movement, are consciously and unconsciously, revealed in the writings of such nineteenth century cemetery enthusiasts and guidebook authors as George Putnam, Wilson Flagg, Henry Dearborn, and Augustus Crafts; and indeed, Forest Hills, by etching and explanation found its way into period literature, wherein the words of authors and architects help to clarify for our twentieth century mind, the intellectual forces at work during this era, which conspired to enculturate, and to culminate in this lovely cemetery.

The Beautification Movement received impetus and ideas from several sources, most significantly: Americans who had traveled in Europe in the 1820s and 1830s; and the philosophies of the Transcendentalists; post-Transcendentalist Art Publicizers; and the nation's Conservatives.   As Americans traveled more and more frequently in Europe, new cultural attitudes emerged as a result of the inevitable, cross-cultural comparisons, and hence, a new assessment of the arts was undertaken, a critical one. Apparently, though for some Americans an uncomfortable one, the prevailing perception of the time was that Europe as a culture had "matured", approaching an apex of sophistication, while America, chronologically, comparatively in its infancy, and hence, commanding a larger store of natural resources, clung to the tenets of rugged individualism, competition, and free enterprise, while Europe embraced the grandeur of a united nation. Many Americans traveling in Europe were reasonably impressed by the rational planning of European cities: They were deliberately irregular, picturesque (4) and human-scaled; but more importantly, they were viewed as representing a collective, societal effort which placed this glory of the nation before the desires of the individual. In contrast, artistically, America was portrayed as disorganized and aesthetically insensitive, since it strongly prioritized individualism, inherently the cause of America's failure to adopt an overall policy of organized, strategic planning in its approach to landscape environments and civic culture.   Surely,   American individualists could and did argue in favor of their own opposing viewpoint, still, particularly in urban centers, the overall feeling was that Europe was capable of planned environmental beauty; and America was not - at least not yet.

Rural cemeteries represent one of the earliest American attempts at planned beautification, an expression of the collective, national, civic pride that travelers had seen in Europe. Mount Auburn, and its offshoot, Forest Hills, became the American response to the European Parks Movement: to France's Pere Lachaise and England's

Regence Park; brethren in spirit, with the motivating forces of the American Parks Movement well-exemplified by Frederic Law Olmstead's later work on the Emerald Necklace of Boston, or the apex of his genius, Grand Central Park in New York City. Cemeteries came into their own, not only as restful residences for the deceased, but as parks adorned with sculptural art, accessible to the living. Cemeteries were planned, public and picturesque.

Travelers to Europe also learned that art and society were related since art could be used for social control. Although initially repelled by religion, particularly Catholicism's, history of psychological manipulation and edification through art, Americans would eventually use art in an analogous manner. As Neil Harris tells us: "All the abstractions about the power of Art to soften brutish feelings and refine the swinish multitudes suddenly drew life." (5) Sensory pleasure, it was reasoned, found in the contemplation of God's creations, Nature especially, led to acquiescence and public security; (6) thus, beauty and social peace became synonyms, and cemeteries reflected these values as ideas learned in Europe, and at home from Transcendentalist writers.

Politics emerged, not merely operationally in the planning of Forest Hills Cemetery; but, as well, in a new way, as the Arts in America reached a new understanding with politics in America: one whose prototype was Europe. From Europe, Americans learned to advocate governmental intervention in favor of the arts, an orientation among the public and private sectors in effect to this day. Metaphorically, first nationally and then locally, the early development of Forest Hills Cemetery and Mayor Henry Dearborn's influence, became an early prototype of public sector involvement in the Arts.(7) American travelers to Europe were also impressed by public accessibility to art(8) and, consequently, cemeteries and parks in America were now opened to the public, which made of them, archetypal examples of the democratization of property in a civil law society, no less than of art, as well.

Not surprisingly, other travelers to Europe returned with opposing convictions. Unlike their compatriots, they were not seduced by European gentility, preferring instead to advocate American rawness, vitality, youth, and intense individualism as virtues. This group of travelers was less easily Anglicized, more inherently capitalistic, and more in tune with Art Advocates here at home. Yet, these travelers would still propose dispersion of art in general, although for different reasons, reasons which catered to particular groups: businessmen, religious leaders, and politicians. Art Advocates appealed to the businessmen on inherently American, innately capitalistic terms: those of profit, betterment, and competition. To the businessman they explained that art would "improve industrial design, increase exports and attract tourists."(9) Further, unlike today, cemeteries were a place for repose, for promenades, for city dwellers to rejuvenate from their workday schedules. Guidebooks allude to the competition not only between cities: a beautiful cemetery increased the desirability and property values of a city; but also of competition with past cultures. Cemetery literature dwells on burial practices of ancient cultures for the legitimization of what was then a novel idea for Americans; but also for competitive reasons: writers and advocates were hesitant to allow modern man to be outdone, to appear unenlightened, and hence, inferior to the ancients. To the politician, Art Advocates promised: "Art would intensify patriotism." (10) This marriage of history, government and reformism found the clearest and strongest expression among the nation's Conservatives. Finally, to the clergy, Art Advocates "demonstrated how art affected morality." (11) What more noble place for this to find expression than in the cemetery movement? The cemetery became an "open air church where Nature's hand alone could dominate." (12)

Transcendentalism was important to the Beautification Movement and its offshoot, the Rural Cemetery Movement, because it stressed reverence for nature, reflection and spiritualism. Contemplation of nature aided self-knowledge. Transcendentalists believed material objects to be emanations of the Divine.(13) To them, a man acquainted with nature was a man acquainted with God.(14) Thoreau spoke of beauty as the "garment of virtue".(15) Beauty, although not an instrument of social control, was a means to fulfillment, the new opiate absorbed in the face of encroaching industrialism. It was symbolic of a people living in harmony and cognizant of the Divine. (16) Ultimately, Transcendentalism offered the stamp of approval to sensory pleasure of the visual persuasion. Within its tenets, visual beauty, an external concept; and spiritual beauty, an internal concept; were united and seen as positive emanations of one universal spirit, not unlike the Neo-Platonic merger of *concetti* and *imago*. Nature reigned supreme and a religious, moral fervor was now added to both governmental and political factions of the Beautification Movement.

The Post-Transcendentalist Art Publicists agreed with most Transcendentalist ideas, yet their point of departure was on the function of art. Art Publicists carried Transcendentalist self-fulfillment several steps further to advocate direct use of art as a means of social control; since not content to merely reflect the earthly existence of Man, Art Publicists sought to reshape him and his society. Publicists saw Art and Beauty as a means to reform, while their predecessors had seen art and beauty, apolitically, as symbolic of pre-existing harmony. In their desire to uphold institutions, Art Publicists were aligned, if with anyone, then with the clergy.

The nation's Conservatives, observing and concerned about the collapse of democratic institutions on various segments of the globe during the 1830s and 1840s advocated a return to views held by America's Founding Fathers. Conservatives felt that the existing formal institutions dedicated to protection of individualism were insufficient; and thus, advocated a wider cultural basis beyond the existing political bases for the protection of individualism and American society, as they attempted to reshape and intensify the "level of virtue, national temper, and the degree of patriotism" (17) indigenous to American culture. Literature of the period, cemetery pamphlets, for example, mention a call to civic pride, which is, in part, pride in government at the local level; and a call to reflection on ancestors and their historical associations, therein, effecting legitimization through reference to history as a means of enlarging their political sphere of influence. Reflective of the desire to extend culturally, that is, to merge and enlarge culture, art, artifact, and intellectual constructs, was the Conservative's need to create symbols of a unified nation, America. How did this manifest itself? Through the erection of monuments by which Conservatives sought visual objectification of positive attitudes toward America. Symbols function in several ways. They proclaim allegiance to a cause often in danger of being forgotten. They merge memory and action, history and present time, and reawaken forgotten thoughts and loyalties. They provide evidence of taste and emotion and their style alludes to the values of the culture which produces them. Although Conservatives were most interested in general monument movements, such as led to the erection of the Washington Monument, the underlying attitudes exactly parallel those espoused in cemetery histories with regard to the functions and appropriateness of memorials, cemetery statues and particular styles of gateways - Greek, Roman, or Egyptian, for example, suitable to cemetery landscape architecture. The erection of certain monuments in particular styles reflected also, the interest in archeology prevalent in the 1830s and 1840s, (18) and the values Americans felt these recently unearthed civilizations, such as

Herculeneum and Vesuvius, represented. Consequently, vaguely incongruous to us today, civic statues tauting Republican values began to appear as adornment to cemetery landscapes in a manner entirely comprehensible to admirers of that time period.

While we have seen that cemeteries such as Forest Hills may be viewed within the framework of the Beautification Movement and its various, attendant, philosophical factions, there are also other interesting perspectives. John Marion, author of <u>Famous and Curious Cemeteries</u>, (19) regards cemeteries as legacies of the past in the sense that their monuments and architectural designs are documentaries of a specific epoch. He, like Albert Fein, believes that cemeteries are parks: horticultural, botanical, arboreal, as well as bird sanctuaries, created to complement and relieve the stress, strain and malaise of everyday industrialized, urban life. Cemeteries also served as museums in which to display sculpture in counties with few public specimens of art, although this may be comparatively less applicable in the Boston area given the existence of the Boston Athenaeum. Further, cemeteries may well have been the only parcel or plot of land that many people would ever own. Perhaps, the strongest catalyst, initially certainly, was the public health advance which cemeteries represented, an idea first popularized by Dr. Jacob Bigelow (who was responsible for Mount Auburn Cemetery); and equally, anthropologically, an advance in how a culture treats its dead.

Within the cemetery literature, Marion presents perhaps the most novel idea for the explanation and justification of cemetery construction. He believes that cemeteries were early examples of town planning, "Victorian necropolii", according to which train of thinking, the public health buildings of towns paralleled the gateway, chapel and offices of cemeteries. In both towns and cemeteries, these edifices were situated along squares or boulevards.

Town mansions, situated on large lots with fashionable drives, found their counterparts in the mausoleums; middle-class homes (tombs) footed winding urban and suburban streets (the walks, avenues, and paths in cemeteries). Some cemeteries also boasted catacombs and columbariums (analogous to town apartment buildings) and "transient accommodations" (mausoleums for rent). (20) Theoretically, cemeteries were social gathering places for the dead no less than social gathering places for the living. Marion mentions the use of cemeteries as entirely appropriate places for promenades, solitary contemplation, family outings, picnics, and for paying homage to the dead. (21). In actual historical practice, it has been said of Forest Hills Cemetery, and further, documented, that on Memorial Day, mausoleums were opened and tea served therein to relatives who wished to commune with deceased family members. I have also been told that Forest Hills Cemetery permitted the grazing of livestock (sheep) and that it was the site of numerous horticultural exhibitions. The notion that horticulture played a part in cemetery activities is clearly intimated by relatively recent photographs of the greenhouses' interiors, old photographs of tropical plants on the grounds, and a stereograph owned by the Boston Athenaeum which represents an amazingly elaborate landscape gardening motif.

Still, there are other important reasons why Forest Hills Cemetery is equally significant and worthy of study. Considered from a dualistic vantage point, as both a rural park and a repository for the deceased, Forest Hills Cemetery assumes a clearly relevant place within the framework of contemporaneous occurrences and developments in landscape architecture, one which represents an understanding of what these choices reveal about: the differences between the nineteenth and twentieth centuries; the changing relationships between America and Europe; the stages of psychological development of America as a nation; the values this work represents; and those of other artistic segments with which it is most closely aligned.

Throughout the preceding pages, we have seen that Forest Hills Cemetery, the physical manifestation of nineteenth century Beautification Drives, reflects the philosophies and special interests of various groups: Transcendentalists, travelers to Europe, Art Advocates, Conservatives; but there may well be another interpretation, previously uncharted, explaining not only the existence and emphasis, but the significance of cemetery preoccupations at this particular time in American history, extending beyond the initial, practical, public health concerns. Just as the basic issues of empiricism and naturalism, truth to nature, the morality of the real, the importance of the object, the democratization of art, the high valuation placed on the factual as emanations of the divine; all reflected the development of painting as it occurred in America in the nineteenth century; so too, are these issues paralleled here, perhaps even more intensely, in the concept of landscape architecture, in this particular cemetery. Which of the two, after all, displays a greater fidelity to Truth? What, as an element of objectification could be more real than not landscape in the artificial sense of one realistically presented in painting as art; but landscape in reality as landscape art?

Nature, in the nineteenth century was more than merely a subject for exploration and presentation, painted on the canvases of the country's artists. It was very significantly that, but more importantly, nature became a vehicle for exploring and representing America's internal and international identity. Superficially, this was most delightfully expressed through the painter's brush, but in a deeper sense the landscape architectural concerns of the cemetery become extensions of those of landscape painting and the ideas associated with its development. In its most tangible, most real sense, the cemetery represents a type of landscape in actuality, pure and simple, one with the least percentage of artifice, and hence is, in nineteenth century terms, the most truly empirical, purist possible expression of the art-object.

Purity, truth, nature, fidelity, the almost divine status of the object, all of which were such important words and concepts for the nineteenth century mind, are no less important to cemetery development than to the other forms of artistic expression. In fact, Trust, God, Man, Nature are concepts as significant to the previous century as technology and industry are all-pervasive and intermeshed with our current century. The "landscape in art" expressed in the form of cemeteries and called landscape architecture differs from "landscape artifice" expressed in the form of painting as object representation, and hence, although previously neglected as a topic for study, is perhaps of all of these arts, closest to the nineteenth century mind in its emphasis on Truth and Fidelity to art and to nature, philosophically and practically.

That nature in the nineteenth century was one vehicle for exploring America's identity as it progressed a single step at a time in her ever-changing, early developmental processes is clear from the time's emphasis on comparison with Europe; the emphasis on social utopianist betterment of Americans societies in rural areas and American cities; both of which trends essentially represent an underlying search for icons of American identity, those symbols by which America may recognize herself and by which other nations may recognize her, clearly, and as a superior. There exists more than the hint of a desire to be the victor in the race for national superiority.

Landscape art, the symbolic epitome of the ideals of nineteenth century America, here in Forest Hills Cemetery, combines the advantages of organized planing which so impressed American travelers to Europe as they sought emulation of European prototypes, yet, still it maintains the characteristically American concepts of democratization, the celebration of the natural world, individuality in design and construction, and eclecticism in the borrowing of architectural prototypes to advance such characteristically American, historical virtues, as may be noted in the use and choice of statuary to advance the concepts of civic pride and Republicanism.

Perhaps the simplest manner in which to clarify the cemetery's place amidst varying trends in painting is merely to ask the hypothetical question: Of the better known nineteenth century landscapists actively painting in America, which would best capture on canvas, that which we understand to be the idea, values and reality of Forest Hills Cemetery? In response to this query, we find ourselves immersed in a paradox of multiple dimensions. Should we chose the naturalistic, spirituality of Hudson River School artist, Asher B. Durand's "Sunset", 1838? The exoticism of a Thomas Cole sunset? Or would Martin Johnson Heade's "Passion Flower and Hummingbirds", 1865/71, be appropriate for representing the spirit of beauty, serenity and floral exotica upon which the gardeners of Forest Hills prided themselves? Or would it be Homer's "Boys In A Pasture"? Most appropriate and appealing to us not only because of its Northeastern Regional setting, but because as does the cemetery, Homer's motif presents monumental human images fixed against a landscape setting as one intended to be read as both pleasurable picture and visual symbol, uncannily similar to the effect of the simple, monumental, Republican figures of the cemetery's statuary rising proudly beneath the Heavens, a tacit acknowledgement of an ontological cosmology in man's relationship to a larger naturalism; and, overall, explore messages which parallel each other in their preservationist attitudes as both present a simplified, symbolic, representation of nostalgic American values of healthy individualism, innocent camaraderie, and idyllic naturalism represented, boy as metaphor to statuary, while both are monuments to an era of pastoral nostalgia, shoulders warmed by the strongest sunlight of the moment of agrarianism before the sun sets for the final time only to rise the next morning, glimpsed for perhaps the last time before the encroachment of industrialism, in that singular moment when the cemetery engages in a celebration of the values of American life.

Considering the unique position of cemetery landscape architecture, we realize that, here, traditional roles between art, artifice and reality reverse themselves: the cemetery represents art and reality, while comparatively, landscape painting embodies art and representation, that is, art and artifice. Forged as well, with the changing thoughts on the nature and type of landscape architecture practiced, is an inherent alteration in the nineteenth century's relationship between Man and Nature: whereas Man has a dominant interest over Nature, as he creates images of nature on the canvas, in landscape architecture, with the emphasis on Romantic aesthetics rather than the imposition of an industrial grid-iron pattern, Nature maintains its autonomy, dominating the environs.

Moreover, the broader cultural developments inherent in landscape painting, gave rise as well to real-life landscape ideals, of which cemeteries became merely the objectification. The mid-nineteenth century was characterized by an emphasis on Nature and landscape which in America found expression in the ideas and writings of Emerson and the Transcendentalists; an expression paralleling well-accepted concepts fervently held abroad and associated with, among others, Wordsworth's emphasis on God and Nature; Snelling's *Naturephilosophie*, Rousseau's natural primitivism; Swedborgianism, spiritualism and Burke's Sublime and Beautiful, and recent author, Rosenbloom's, the Northern Romantic Tradition. Incorporated herein is an across the board respect for Nature; and a new concept of Nature coinciding with the changing concept of landscape painting away from academic classicism toward pure, direct representation of the beauty, empirical topography, and spirit of the land itself, devoid of historical reference, as with Frederic Church's paintings. Later in the century, this evolves into the landscape painting of Europe's Objective Naturalism (c.f. Sloane), and subsequently, Impressionism; while in America, it is more strongly tied to pure landscape as the embodiment of geographical specificity and the nationalistic ideals of a distinct American identity whose spiritual and expansionary inclinations were categorically expressed by its earliest journalist explorers.

Support for the notion that a commonality of thought between the characteristically sensitized nineteenth century merger of Aesthetics and Ethics exists between Dearborn, creator of Forest Hills Cemetery; Olmstead, the father of American landscape tradition; Jacob Bigelow, the principal designer of Mount Auburn (Forest Hills' sister cemetery); writers such as Emerson, Thoreau, Ruskin,

Wordsworth, Whitman, Bryant; and landscape painters such as Bierstadt, Church, and Cole is gleaned from each one's parallel appreciation of such tellingly distinct variables as: a reverence for romantic nature best espoused by Edmund Burke's polarities of the sublime and the beautiful; stylistic similarities; the courageous palliation of art's democratization effected in principle from the heritage of Jacksonian democracy amidst a milieu comprised of emerging patronage aristocracies spawned in America in the latter segment of the century; an immanent love of the land, especially its open vistas, as it is translated into a vital force, symbolic of American power and potency, arising out of the legacy of Jeffersonian agrarianism; and the seemingly innocent, intermingling of some curiously coincidental tidbits of biographical information.

Among the writers of the 1850s, reverence for the land, its glorification in American thought was embraced as a means for America to turn away from the feudal past of Europe to build a new order founded upon Nature, a sort of Americanizing of America, an initial step in the formation of a national identity - an idea also appealing to painters of landscape. This need represented a longing for an American identity presupposed as superior to assimilation of European models and one which advocated open vistas, and American strength, in its celebration of the virgin land of the paintings of the West, and analogously, the open spaces remaining in the more densely settled East, places like Grand Central Park, Forest Hills, Mount Auburn, and the Emerald Necklace. While landscape artists were tied to a sometimes political, often apolitical or rather non-partisan, nationalist spirit in the West; in the East, the landscape architecture artists were imbued with a strain of social utopianism spurred by Parke Godwin, and later, by the antebellum principle that the public good was central to the well-being of society; common to all of which was a search for the comparative, competitive betterment of America.

In an attempt to clarify his own concept of Nature, in a presentation in New York, Olmstead referred to Albert Bierstadt's "Domes of Yosemite" to illustrate his contention that:

> The first point to be kept in mind, then, is the
> preservation and maintenance as exactly as possible,
> of the natural scenery. (22)

a sentiment which coincides with those of Ruskin, Wordsworth,
Thoreau and Emerson; the landscapists; and the goals of Utopian
Socialist environmental planners, as was Olmstead; which were
supported, first by New York's cultural elite, then Boston's, and
which as a group sought humanitarian social reform by using
nature aesthetically, as an escape from the city; moralistically, as a
quieter of the multitudes of oppressed workers living in tenement
houses; and politically, as a democratic instrument, well-suited
to improving the city by improving its public institutions; ideas
essentially in opposition to the popular style of Richard Morris
Hunt's European-imported, French classically inspired, Beaux Arts
Style; but well-suited to Olmstead and Dearborn.

As a cemetery Forest Hills was a remarkable improvement over
the practical, utilitarianism of its Boston predecessors: cemeteries
such as those at King's Chapel and Burial Grounds at the corner
of Tremont and School Streets, or Copps Hill Cemetery, or Phipps
Street Cemetery, and their limited space and equally limited
concept of burial as the mere demarcation of the event of physical
death, the terminus marking a rite of passage; distinct from the
rural cemetery's extended contemplation of death and the positive
reminiscences spurred by the surrounding aesthetic beauty there;
and in its role as a rural park, the celebration of life.

Considered as a rural park, as an example of landscape architecture,
created in the nineteenth century in Boston, our thoughts naturally
turn most readily toward the work and influence of Frederick
Law Olmstead; since not only was he the acknowledged father of
landscape architecture in America; but also, because he designed
the Emerald Necklace, between two important segments of which

Franklin Park and Jamaica Pond, is located our lovely gem, Forest Hills Cemetery.

Categorized as a rural cemetery, Forest Hills is readily associated, in the Boston area, with its sister cemetery, Mount Auburn Cemetery; but it is equally interesting as a manifestation of the rural park as it existed this side of the river in Boston, a precursor in time, yet a contemporary in spirit of Olmstead's systematized Boston park plan, often touted as the most eloquent expression of the schematized romantic park of the nineteenth century. Indeed, we may glean a kindredness of spirit between Olmstead's ideas for Boston and Dearborn's ideas for Forest Hills. Stylistically, we recognize in Forest Hills, the elements of a nineteenth century romantic park in association with Olmstead's concept of the romantic, in many of its features including: the basic idea of formal landscaping, skillfully imposed upon human-scaled space imbued with emotional content; the emphasis on pre-existing, natural contours enhanced by blending, and accents, composed of natural materials; the planned concept of space as one to be experienced on foot or by virtue of the slow meanderings of a horsedrawn carriage; repeated use of submerged landscape patterns and colors echoed in building materials; dualistic accommodation of traffic by footpaths for pedestrians, bridle paths and carriageways for slightly speedier methods of locomotion; the thematic uniting of buildings through the use of similar architectural styles and similar compositional materials; relatively unpretentious gateways with either direct walking access or a moderately formal structural entranceway; and an eclectic, contemporary marriage of the timeless English cottage style with historical architectural renderings tauting the new discoveries of history associated with the unearthing of archeological sites (Herculeneum and Visuvius). Other similarities between Olmsteadian concepts and those of Dearborn include: the use of groves of trees to act as sound (wind and visual) barriers shielding the park and its visitors from the disturbing sights and sounds of the city; wide open spaces with long vistas; winding avenues and sporadic clusterings of coniferous and deciduous trees in groves which allowed for natural thinning; an overall scheme geared toward passive enjoyment rather than the active recreation associated with New York's Central Park or Boston's Franklin Park; a reverence for the particular manner in which death is conceptualized and experienced as a poetic event dignified by peaceful surroundings and immortalized literarily by epitaphs on headstones as a sort of metaphor for the cemetery's dedication speech; and various common structures associated with it: the inclusion of lakes to mirror heavenly skies; a system of underground drains similar to those Olmstead used in New York's Central Park (23) to accommodate runoff and maintain moisture in soil conditions appropriate for particular species of plants; as reflects a burgeoning of certain types of new knowledge born of applications initiated by gentlemen farmers; and incidental accents conceived in the Olmsteadian tradition, including naturally occurring botanical specimens characteristic of the surrounding climate, to which Dearborn added exotica: all integrated into the city milieu so as to encourage pleasant, rural enjoyments. In addition, Dearborn's interest in preventive maintenance, the perpetual care of Forest Hills Cemetery, paralleled Olmstead's concern and provision for park maintenance; both being precursors to a later, historical preservation movement, and eventually, to the planning of cities, presaging the acceptance of Ecology as a science.

Inconsistent with Olmsteadian romantic landscape tradition, but utilized by Dearborn at Forest Hills Cemetery were ornamental ironwork gateways and fences surrounding the lots in a manner replicating the metal encirclements of city architecture found in such older areas of Boston as Louisburg Square and Winthrop Square; (24) as well as the use of exotic plants; both of which Olmstead and Bigelow viewed as traitors to the romantic naturalist cause in their evocation of exoticism, luxury and the upper-class, aristocratic, European associations of the contemporaneously counter-current, Beaux Arts movement, best exemplified by Richard Morris Hunt's French classically inspired, regal presentations of both building and landscape architecture, such as Biltmore in North Carolina or Richardson's New York Capital Building. (25) Still, Dearborn's interest in exotic plants, for which he planned and constructed ample greenhouses and conservatories with sophisticated underground reservoirs, may represent an interest not in the Beaux

Arts style, nor in aristocratic bearing, but instead, the pervading fascination with the new concept of species, associated with the times' interest in such newly published books as Darwin's <u>Origin of Species</u>, Audubon's ornithological prints, or even Olmstead's own plan for an arboretum of different species of trees - the Arnold Arboretum; or his plans for variously infused rose gardens in the Fenway segment of the Emerald Necklace, all of which speak to the popular interest in diversity at mid-century, as well as local designers interests in gentleman farming which boasted a long and prestigious, if sporadic, legacy in America.

Olmstead and Downing enjoyed Jeffersonian thought which sought the fulfillment of a particular democratic destiny, unlike that of any European nation. The essential aspiration of Olmstead's group, like that of Jefferson's, was for America to develop a distinctly superior, yet homogeneous and harmonious civilization to serve as an example for the divided and warring continent of Europe underlying which homogeneity and democracy was a search for the commonalties inherent in a unified national identity and national spiritual and political unity, as a means to assert a sense of international superiority. Landscape art and landscape architecture with a distinctly American accent was an ideal means to fulfill these desires.

Beyond all three gentleman's adherence to Jeffersonian thought, as we consider Olmstead's and Downing's influence on Dearborn, of ancillary significance, yet contributory, we recall such operational level, biographical details as Olmstead's own love of the land, and his burning drive to complete the good works of a beneficent discipline. Prior to his career as a landscape architect, up until 1850, Olmstead was engaged in farming. Later in the century, he joined Downing, to advocate for the formation of a scientific, agricultural college which would include botanical pursuits, scientific preservation, and a betterment of the general and scientific education of farmers and agriculturists, hoping to imbue in them, the spirit of preservation, as a foothold on the inclinations of the next generation of Americans. We recall also, Olmstead's use of Bierstadt's painting, "The Domes of Yosemite", as an example of the type of Romantic Nature, Nature unspoiled, open land, the ever-residual retinal image of his psyche, from which he translated the content of his work from its most propitious, profound source - his own mind's eye. Olmstead's protege on the nearby Arnold Arboretum Project was Charles Eliot, son of Harvard College's President. More importantly, though there was Llewellyn Park, America's first conceived suburb planned in the Romantic Style, completed by Andrew Jackson Davis, a precedent for the work of Olmstead; partly because its designer influenced Olmstead, stylistically; partly because Davis was such a close friend of Downing; partly because Calvert Vaux, Olmstead's lifelong friend and collaborator had also been Downing's Assistant during his tenure as architect of Llewellyn Park development. That Bigelow, with whom Dearborn worked at Mount Auburn, looked to Olmstead, is clear, stylistically, and in such details as his reasoning for the removal of iron fences around the lots, as inappropriately territorial, and not in keeping with the sense of democracy and brotherhood which should rightly be advanced in this particular type of landscape architecture.

In the sphere of landscape architecture, the differences between the nineteenth century and the twentieth are essentially the discrepancies between, on the one hand, agrarianism, democracy, the perspectival, the human-scaled and humanly-cognizant, the unified and universal, the ambulatory, and the ontologically spiritual; and on the other hand, the secular, the dynamic, the technological, the spatially disjunctive, the toweringly monumental, automation and anomie. Still, common to both of these centuries was an increasing urbanism to which both responded differently in terms of style; while yet similarly, in their attempt to recognize a convergent problem, one potentially solvable by a return to Nature and the creation of certain types of space; and their consequent merger of Aesthetics and Ethics, beneath the banner of an agreed upon goal of advancing the humanity of humankind: humankinship thoughout not merely the inevitable event of death but a life of aspirations. Although its longevity and construction activity broaches the twentieth century *and* the nineteenth century, Forest Hills Cemetery, a distinctly important cultural contribution, is a cultural phenomenon of the nineteenth century. Forest Hills Cemetery relates not merely to religion and nature, and to the life and death of its subscribers, but to the life and death of a symbol of American identity - the romantic landscape; and as a nineteenth century landscape architectural phenomenon, having glanced backward to the poetic and architectural heritage of prior centuries, it as well, looks forward to the metropolitan planning of the twentieth century and to the life and death of America's cities.

In conclusion, in response to the question: Wherein lies the significance of the existence of the cultural artifact, the cemetery, within the confines of nineteenth century American society?: we realize that the cemetery is perhaps the sole physical manifestation, and decidedly the most remarkably complex, singular artifact, a system embracing sculpture, the decorative arts, Aesthetics, Landscape Architecture and Urban Planning in a fashion in which are negotiated and settled this era's resolution of its own major aesthetic conflicts, emanating from those very first dialogues between artists, philosophers, literary men, businessmen, medical men, religious and spiritual leaders and Republicans, as included such issues as those of: art and artifice, the secular and the spiritual, the temporal and the intransitory, God and Man, artistic truth and aesthetic artifice, representation and fabrication. No other artifact of nineteenth and perhaps twentieth century America hints at and broaches so many issues, so completely, so confidently, so universally, so well - so unexpectedly, subtly, and uniquely as Forest Hills Cemetery.

SECTION I:

FOREST HILLS CEMETERY: THE CULTURAL-PHILOSOPHICAL CONTEXT

1.   Neil Harris, The Artist in American Society: The Formative Years,
     1790-1860. George Brasilia (New York: 1966) p. 201;and Albert
     Fein, "The American City: The Ideal and the Real", in Edgar
     Kaufman, The Rise of American Architecture. Metropolitan
     Museum and Praegar (New York: 1970), p. 81-84.

2-18. Harris, Ibid., respectively, #2 - 188; #3 - 156-159; #4 - 16; #5 - 159;
     #6 - 160; #7 - 162; #8 - 162; #9, #10, #11 - 167; #12 - 201; #13 - 172;
     #14 - 173; #15 - 181; #16 - 179.

19.   For discussion, see John F. Marion's Famous and Curious
     Cemeteries, Crown Publishers (New York: 1977), p. xii, 56-58, 3-10.

20-21. Marion, Ibid., p. xii,

22.   Albert Fein. Frederick Law Olmstead and The Environmental
     Tradition. George Brasilia (New York: 1972), Note to Plate 30.

23.   Fein. Ibid., Note to Plate 94.

24.   The Boston Society of Architects, Architecture Boston. Barre
     Publishing. (Massachusetts: 1976) Text by Joseph L. Eldridge.

25.   Heckser, August. Open Spaces: The Life of American Cities.
     Harper and Rowe. (New York: 1977).

SECTION II:

THE ART HISTORICAL NICHE

Section II:

The Art Historical Niche

Forest Hills from the art historical, visual standpoint? Considered within this context, Forest Hills Cemetery is an indirect translation of the concept of landscape architecture presented by John Nash's Regence Park in London. This park reflects the ideas of Sir Henry Repton, understandably, since Nash and Repton were once partners. Repton's theories were transmitted to America through the writings of Andrew Jackson Downing and had at their core, the operative idea that land could be "scientifically planned according to use and the natural potential of the site." (1) This implied: a positive value to cultivated open spaces; (2) stimulated arboreal enhancements; and essentially constituted the antithesis of the grid pattern of land development which had been heretofore characteristic of American landscape theory. All of these, novel concepts at that time, found expression in Forest Hills Cemetery as Downing, Repton and Nash advocated opposition to the mindless imposition of an arbitrary pattern of perpendicular avenues, favoring instead a design in which land use retained its irregular passages, picturesque identity, and individuality. By consenting to this design change, participants embraced a reorientation in the relationship between Man and

Nature, so that now manmade developments enhanced but did not overpower the basic profile of the land. Forest Hills Cemetery well illustrates this point in the method of avenue development employed, for here, avenues were made to wind around hills, often defining the base and culminating in one or a series of loops at the summit, one effect being that according to indigenous intentions, original tree groupings, interesting rock outcroppings, and natural terraces were permitted to remain intact.

Art historically, one prototype for Forest Hills Cemetery was Mount Auburn Cemetery in Cambridge, which is in turn believed to have been modeled in function if less so in design on Pere Lachaise cemetery in Paris. (3) Mount Auburn represents the first major rural cemetery established in the United States. (4) It was the objectification of ideas espoused by Dr. Jacob Bigelow, the man credited with initiating the American Cemetery Movement. Working alongside Bigelow on the Mount Auburn project was Henry A. S. Dearborn, who would later provide the major impetus for the establishment of Forest Hills, the establishment and progress of which bears certain similarities to Mount Auburn, if indeed the stylistic outcome differs.

Both Forest Hills and Mount Auburn shared their era's reaction against existing methods of dealing with the dead: methods which were deemed inappropriate from the standpoint of public health and morality. A physician by training, Mount Auburn's Jacob Bigelow was first to complain about the "promiscuous concentration of members" that is, of bodies of the congregation and the Commonwealth, buried in vaults or old cemeteries in crowded parts of the city or church cellars.(5) Later, in his attempt to secure a cemetery in Roxbury, its mayor, John C. Clark, would point out that Boston's Eustis Street and Warren Street cemeteries were dilapidated and full: that "Mount Auburn is too remote"; and that "comparatively few feel able to procure lots there" (6). To the public health issues was added the aesthetic issue by Augustus Crafts who tells us: "Each year the burials have become more numerous and from this constant increase in the mode of burial... such cemeteries in the midst of the living are prejudicial to health as well as disagreeable to the eye". (7) Eventually, hopes for a new cemetery became political fodder as is revealed in an exerpt from "An Address to the Citizens of Boston and Vicinity" (8) which adds to the public health issue the assumptions of civic pride and governmental responsibility:

> Every one of our cemeteries is already full to an extent which, in greater and less degree is prejudicial to the public health. Indeed, during the prevalence of epidemic, it became necessary to disuse several of our burial grounds, not merely on account of offensive exhalations, but for want of actual space for additional interments. This state of things is discreditable to Boston and inconsistent with due regard to the safety of its citizens.

In response to these problems, advocates of both cemeteries held the image of rural burial as ideal. Crafts, writing on Forest Hills, informs us that:

> the establishment of ornamental cemeteries in the vicinity of large towns was but the cultivation of a refined taste and reverent regard for the dead which had hitherto found expression chiefly in simple rural life. (9)

Here we see a reaction against the gloomy Puritan burial which failed to beautify the grave and thereby failed to encourage remembrance or visits,(10) and which failed as well to assimilate the increasing American lure of materialism and ostentation expressed by ornamentation. It was Edward Everett's 1832 essay, "The Proposed Rural Cemetery",(11) originally referring to Mount Auburn, which supplied the ideal visual image. His concept of appropriate burial, internalized from his time, extends into the American psyche as:

> beneath the shade of a venerable tree, on the slope of the verdant lawn, and within the seclusion of the forest; removed from all the discordant scenes of life...

In their public explanations, advocates of both cemeteries described at length, the ancient burial customs of the Greeks, Egyptians, Turks, and other ancient civilizations (12) which in part reflected the time's interest in archeology; in part, an attempt at legitimizing a new idea through associations with past authority; and, in part, a guide for the development of the cemeteries themselves.

Participants in both cemetery's campaigns, espoused similar benefits to be derived from development of these cemeteries. The nature of these benefits was multi-faceted: psychological, emotional, religious, and county oriented. A mourner could "indulge his grief or find consolation for his sorrow amid the beauties of nature".(13) He could enjoy Nature's handiwork intermingled with man's influence, and the "associations of memory...The effect, is both tranquilizing and inspiring." (14) Both Forest Hills and Mount Auburn were presented as places for serious meditation where one might: "ponder those themes neglected by the multitude during the hurry of business or in the idle 'whirl of pleasure'". (15) They were places where grief and insecurity could be quieted by the land; thus indulging the American psyche in its preoccupation with land as space, refuge, power, and wealth.

> The trees, the flowers, the still waters, and the green
> landscape, allied as they are with the themes of
> poetry, with our ideas of heaven, and with the hopes
> of our immortality, soften our grief into a tender
> melancholy, and quiet the anxieties of faith. (16)

Cemeteries also provided a means to quiet other anxieties. Here, a man could "deposit the mortal remains of his friends, and ...provide a place of burial for himself, which, while living, he may contemplate without dread or disgust;...which is secure from intrusion, surrounded with everything that can fill the heart with emotion."(17) Both Forest Hills and Mount Auburn were places where men could know God reflected through rural settings; where memories of persons past would give rise to reveries, and to patriotism and pride which would in turn benefit the community. Nature reflected a call to the contemplation of spiritualism; civic statues, a call to arms as mirrored national values; and the biographical backgrounds of the interred, a call to literature: all part and parcel of an oasis of tranquility amidst a desert of urban madness.

Besides sharing goals and benefits, campaign strategies, and the concept of a rural ideal, Mount Auburn and Forest Hills had in common corporate structure, patterns of land acquisition, choice of essential architectural structures, elements of style, choice of topography and process of land development. While Mount Auburn had a Board of Managers and subcommittees, Forest Hills had its Board of Comissioners and committees: the common denominator seated on both boards was member, Henry Dearborn. At Mount Auburn, Jacob Bigelow had been the catalyst: at Forest Hills, Dearborn reigned. At Mount Auburn, Dearborn's committee had been responsible for clearing avenues, grading ground, laying out roads, superintending workmen, transplanting trees from his (Dearborn's) own land; (18) so it was hardly surprising that Dearborn later filled an analogous function at Forest Hills. Bigelow had named avenues, paths and ponds after natural objects at Mount Auburn, usually tree and flower titles: Dearborn would follow suit at Forest Hills. In fact, many of the names exactly correspond, testimony to the literary naturalism of the era. Both Auburn and Forest Hills incorporated, although for different reasons. Both reached the decision that lots had to be sold with the provision for the future - perpetual care; in keeping with the preservationist spirit which the new discipline of landscape architecture held dear as an essential ethos. Both relied on outside help for their initial funding: Mount Auburn was assisted by the Massachusetts Horticultural Society, which relied on subscription and auction to raise money; while Forest Hills was assisted by the local town government which issued notes. Further, Forest Hills received assistance from two of its future Comissioners who bought land in anticipation of aid from the government. One of the two was Dearborn.

Stylistically, the topography of Mount Auburn is severe and spectacular: Forest Hills is more sedate. In both instances, the original land was farmland comprised of rolling hills, unexpected ridges, low lying areas, intimate dells, quaint wooded groves, and panoramic vistas. Mount Auburn originally possessed water bodies, whereas Forest Hills' main body of water, Lake Hibiscus, was manmade to supplement a rudimentary water system in existence in the nineteenth century. Essentially, these two rural cemeteries represent opposing aesthetic viewpoints quintessential to the era's preoccupation with Burke and the sublime and the beautiful. Rather than a tangential compromise, we find a dichotomous understanding with Mount Auburn representing the sublime polarity, Forest Hills symbolizing the opposing loci of the contemplatively beautiful.

The natural outcroppings of each cemetery were fairly faithfully retained and enhanced as was much of the original vegetation, which included native deciduous and coniferous trees and shrubs, to which later was added, through the efforts of Dearborn, imported ornamental trees and shrubs. Rhododendrons, in particular, crept steadily into the overall scheme. In both instances, cemetery design utilized trees in an analogous fashion: tall rows of long-standing pines screened out the city; arbor vitae framed monuments; deciduous trees were interspersed among the graves for shade and ambiance, and to form arches and avenue borders, as if overshadowing green umbrellas of God or grief metaphorically pointing ever upward toward the heavens for release. Both cemeteries exhibited an additive pattern of land acquisition, beginning with one large, major section; followed by the seriated purchase of additional land directly along its periphery; in keeping with the notion that expansion was a positive virtue.

Architecturally, corresponding structures may be found in each of the cemeteries, as the essentials needed to be considered respectable included: a formal main gateway; receiving tombs, a chapel and a business office, an ironwork fence bordering the entire periphery, and an observation tower which functioned as a landmark while also affording a panoramic view of neighboring towns. Both cemeteries contained temporary wooden structures, sanded and painted to resemble stone, until stone edifices could be substituted.

With respect to avenue development, both cemeteries for pragmatic considerations viewed this as a major priority, and toward this end, each retained the autonomy of the original landscape, by using a design plan of winding avenues to form an inter-connected maze, thus effecting a combination of autonomy and utilitarianism in avenue design, as avenues tended toward the curvilinear, in opposition to the gridpattern; while paths acquiesced to the geometric grid pattern so as to join avenues on the perpendicular axis, an overall economic purpose being served: a sparing organization facilitating the sale and care of the lots. In addition, Forest Hills appears to have larger areas of broad, flat fields of grids, particularly along the western border (now Canterbury Street), where the land was purchased later. Early sections of the cemetery, notably its eastern section, are far hillier, corresponding more closely to Mount Auburn's topography. That Mount Auburn's avenues do not exhibit so extensive a dependence upon the methodology of the grid pattern, as does Forest Hills, is clearly noted on historical and current maps.

On balance, the differences between Forest Hills and Mount Auburn are comparatively less in number than their similarities. To begin with, Forest Hills maintinated a public section along Canterbury Street, where in accordance with the Acts of establishing the cemetery, Roxbury residents could be buried free of charge; a *quid quo pro* arrangement reflecting the assistance received from the city government, which had issued city notes to the cemetery, enabling the necessary land to be purchased; thereby initiating a courtesy to residents, common practice in many towns to date. Mount Auburn, having no similar tie to Cambridge municipal government, had no government subsidized public interments. Secondly, Forest Hills' "Board of Comissioners" was elected by the local government, at least until 1868, when the cemetery incorporated on the eve of Roxbury's annexation to Boston. Thirdly, biographical histories reveal that most persons associated with and buried within Forest Hills Cemetery had lived lives revolving around business and science whereas Mount Auburn's clientele was composed predominantly of "men of letters". (19) Finally, although Dearborn was associated with both cemeteries until his death in the early 1850s, his role at Forest Hills was significantly more active, since here he was at once the initial catalyst, designer of events and paths, designer of the

Egyptian gateway, the main entrance, the initial gateway as gave rise to public impressions, and general overseer.

Aesthetics assumes an active role in the conception, execution, and interpretation of these two cemeteries, and in their stylistic analysis as well, just as aesthetics played a major role in nineteenth century thought and action. Nineteenth century American society held dear, the concept of an ontological cosmology - a divinely created world; and its logical derivations: an harmonious Nature organized according to universal laws from which inspirational source of knowledge intelligible Man could deduce - intents, values, processes; succinctly - an exemplary template according to which system of design and function - he, himself might discover the underlying principles of natural law according to which he might organize his life, his society, his times, and his artistic symbols. Both Forest Hills Cemetery and Mount Auburn Cemetery fit neatly into this nineteenth century aesthetic cachet, even in their differences, for Forest Hills clearly typifies one side of an important typology while Mount Auburn exemplifies its diametrical counterpart. Throughout the nineteenth century, Man and Nature assumed dynamic interrelationships: Nature's divine template could be a model for man's social organization; Nature could be purist as a source of an aesthetic response; Nature could harbor the moral forces of good and evil particularly through its effect on men's emotions. Aestheticians penned many a paragraph on these individual themes, yet one philosopher in particular, impacted Western Aesthetics with a force and congeniality unmatched for generations. One philosopher successfully combined all the most important themes into a cogent treatise which was to have far-reaching effects on our own thoughts about Art, and life and how we perceive and respond to the world. This philosopher was Edmund Burke; his seminal treatise "A Philosophical Inquiry Into the Origin of Our Ideas of the Sublime and the Beautiful". (20)

The importance of this discourse rests with: its truth; its universality to basic human thought; its typology of Nature with a majuscule "N", as delineated dichotamously; while retaining the essence of the nineteenth century's basic cosmology - its preoccupation with an omniscient, omnipotent God. Essentially, Forest Hills exists as a Burkian icon of contemplative, beautiful nature, while Mount Auburn embodies its opposite: sublime, awesome Nature. Both adhere to the contemporaneous American Transcendentalist and emerging Northern Romatnic Traditions in Europe and their concept of humankind's corrrect relationship with Nature as non-interventionist and respectful, even subservient. Outside of native AmericanIndianculture,thisreverencerepresentsarelativeanomalie prior to the preservationist movement and environmentalism of and subsequent to, Olmstead. Both cemeteries exist as a reaction against previously accepted ideas on the relationship with Nature as one characterized by dominance, by imposition of Man's hand atop God's through cultivated techniques associated with earlier English landscape architecture theorists, and the formal, geometric programmesofEnglishgardens. ForestHillsCemeteryinitsserenity, the more beautiful, evokes sentiments of sedate, peaceful harmony; whereas Mount Auburn impresses as more sublime, appealing to our sense of awe, the magnificent, even the forebodingly spectacular as we imagine thunder and lightening and the spectacular effects of Nature's spiritual presence traversing its personna. Indeed, if Mount Auburn be the thunderclap, Forest Hills emerges as its rainbow. Such impressions are technically derived: the sublime Mount Auburn is replete with dramatic sweeps of landscape, strong contrasts of texture among its more massive arboreal groupings, spectacular areas of deep darkness, abrupt topographical changes, recessions, and counterpoint turns, whereas Forest Hills presents as more smoothly and wholly unified with gently rolling transitions and relatively more shallow terracing. Indeed, Mount Auburn, as well, has its classically sedate, light kissed area, most notably that section supporting the rectangular reflecting pool as barely ripples nearby its stunning Greek Mausoleums, making of it a microcosmic *forte* of Burkian duality.

Section II:
The Art-historical Niche

1. John F. Marion. Famous and Curious Cemeteries. Crown
    Publishers. (New York: 1977) p. xii, 3-10, 56-58.

2. Albert Fein, "The American City: The Ideal and the Real", in
    Edgar Kaufman, The Rise of AmericanArchitecture. Metropolitan
    Museum and Praegar (New York: 1970) p. 81-84.

3. Fein. Ibid., p. 81, 82.

4. Jacob Bigelow. A History of Mount Auburn Cemetery. James
    Monroe and Company (Bosto: 1860), p. 128.

5. Frank Foxcroft. Mount Auburn Cemetery. James Monroe and
    Company (Boston; n.d.) p. 419.

6. William Agustus Crafts. Forest Hills Cemetery: Its Establishment,
    Progress, Scenery, Monuments. John Backup Pres. (Roxbury:
    1855), p. 18.

7. Crafts. Ibid., p. 8.

8. Francis O. Watts, Albert Fearing, John H. Wilkins. An Address
    to the Citizens of Boston and Vicinity on the Subject of a Rural
    Cemetery. Eastburn's Press (Boston: 1859).

9. Crafts. Op.cit., p. 5.

10. Crafts. Ibid, p. 6.

11. Edward Everett. "The Proposed Rural Cemetery", in Jacob
    Bigelow, A History of Mount Auburn Cemetery, James Munroe
    and Company (Boston: 1860), p. 128.

12. For discussion, see Bigelow, A History of Mount Auburn
    Cemetery; Henry Dearborn, September 6, 1847, Joint Standing
    Coittee on Burial Grounds; and Crafts, Ibid, p. 4.

13. Crafts. Op.cit., p. 13.

14. Focroft, Mount Auburn, p. 438.

15. Foxcroft, Ibid., p. 438.

16. Wilson Flagg, <u>Mount Auburn: Its Scenes, Its Beauties, and Its Lessons</u>, James Monroe and Company (Boston: 1861), p. 8 and 9.

17. Edward Everett. <u>Op.cit.</u>, p. 138.

18. Jacob Bigelow. <u>Op.cit.</u>, p. 20.

19. Interview with Neil Savage, week of the meeting of November 15, 1979 at Forest Hills Cemetery.

20. Edmund Burke, "An Inquiry into the Origins of Our Ideas of the Beautiful and Sublime", in <u>The Harvard Classics. Vol. 24</u>, P.F. Collier and Son (New York: 1967).

SECTION III:

OVERVIEW TO THE JOURNAL

SECTION III

OVERVIEW TO THE JOURNAL

A chronological overview (1) of the progress and history of Forest Hills Cemetery reveals that the decade of the eighteen-forties, the beginning, was characterized by organizational and developmental stages in politics, personnel and planning: in all spheres of which activities, Henry Dearborn played a key role. Although not the first to recognize the need for a cemetery in the Roxbury area, politically polished, Mayor Dearborn was the catalyst who succeeded in pushing the concept of Forest Hills Cemetery through political channels until its establishment was ensured. His ability to create and maintain relationships with City Council members, Committee members, the Board of Comissioners, and his choice of cemetery personnel, especially Brims, were all crucial to the success of his project. As a result of his political *savoir faire*, Forest Hills Cemetery moved from concept to construction.

As operational manager and conceptual chief, Dearborn contributed significantly since based on his background as a landscape architect and his prior experience at Mount Auburn Cemetery, he was well prepared by experience and training to create the overall landscape design - the zones, hills, and lakes, to champion the engineering projects such as the steam pumps, the draining systems connecting the lakes, and to propose the appropriate sequence of land acquisitions, taking into account the form and function and design possibilities of each segment with respect to integration into the ultimate end: a unified whole.

In his planning of the zones, Dearborn began by taking into account the land's various natural features, retaining and embellishing each site's own hills and outcroppings, designing the open areas and flat fields suitable for division into burial lots, the functional mecca and cash cow of the operation, outlining plans for creating and excavating the man-made lakes, a landscape architectural phenomenon for the time and region, and creating the systems for connecting these new lakes with the cemetery's existing ones.

An engineer by profession, by temperament, a man cognizant of health and aesthetics, Dearborn was first to broach certain engineering concepts which mirrored both his concerns. He proposed, for example, the use of a steam pump and interconnected network of metallic, underground pipelines, which would facilitate water flow between the lakes, thereby reducing stagnation and ensuring consistent water levels in all water bodies throughout the summer's drier months. Further, his system provided water for the beautiful cascades between Lake Dell and Woodbine Mere, and for the water fountains in each of the lakes. His system resolved the problem of periodic drainage, necessitated by landscape alterations, excavation and enlargement, and structural repairs to the pond walls.

Construction activities in the early years naturally revolved around providing the basics: securing the land (from Seaverns, Parkinson, and Warren), making it accessible by constructing carriage avenues and footpaths within the cemetery, thus facilitating movement among the various sections, necessary for opening up the first fields; and trenching, showing and selling the first lots. During this first decade, the nursery was started and lodges for Superintendent Brims and the gatekeeper were constructed. The cemetery entrances, including Dearborn's Egyptian Main Gateway on Parkinson's land, and the two secondary entrances on Walk Hill and Canterbury Avenues, were created, enlivened, and enhanced. Then, it was during the eighteen-forties that the cemetery's basic landscape architectural elements: those important first steps toward combining aesthetics and function, as if leaping unharnessed from Dearborn's mind, began to take visible shape.

The decade of the fifties brought continued expansion, more land purchases and the creation of a new town, West Roxbury, which actually included Forest Hills Cemetery, but from which the cemetery would remain distinct as a result of political maneuverings. The faces on the Board of Comissioners changed significantly due to death: with Dearborn's and Coleman's passing, and the resignation of Superintendent Brims yet amidst this loss the future aspirations of the cemetery were not lost. The cemetery's appearance was permanently, beautifully enhanced by extensive work on Lake Hibiscus, a man-made lake, created and changed through countless excavations and enlargements, and the creation of its two man-made islands, Swan and Spring Island, both of which produced a topography so popular and attractive, that a cemetery omnibus had to be established to shuttle visitors to the new creations, and the lake was ordered fenced-in as a precautionary measure since visitors had become so frequent, suggesting that the grounds were considered a bonafide rural park for the multitudes, not merely a restricted haven for the deceased where their handfuls of loved ones might visit. Attention was also given to the Walk Hill Entrance and the various fields: MacPhelah, Manoah, Ephron; while the first two structural developments, including two large receiving tombs at Lake Dell, a greenhouse and two additional tenements - one for the new Superintendent Moulten and a blacksmith shop, were completed. As a result of the various land acquisitions, by the middle of this decade, examination of spatial statistics tell us that this cemetery/rural park had grown to encompass an impressive approximate 105 acres.

During the sixties, with Dearborn gone, the Board of Comissioners began to rely more seriously on outside architectural firms such as Kendall and Wood, and Brookline's Mr. Panter, thus laying the groundwork for similar trends to follow in the next two decades, when Commissioners turned to important architects, Emerson and Fehmer, and Van Brundt and Howe. While the early years of the decade brought completion of Lake Hibiscus, exclusive of minor embellishments, the middle years were significant for progress on Panter's Gothic Gateway located at the Main Entrance. Throughout this entire decade, expansion continued though land purchases from Peters, Seaverns, Warren, Williams, Simmons and several of I. Cary. The Soldier's Lot, for veterans of the Civil War, a larger stable, a tenement, and a more sophisticated greenhouse, renamed the Conservatory, appeared to house the tropical shrubbery, which increasingly more popular, made their appearance.

Throughout the seventies, the cemetery benefited again from increasingly larger land purchases: first 37 acres, then 28 acres, and the inclusion of increasingly more beautiful architectural structures. Refined, dignified and yet utilitarian, best describe Emerson and Fehmer's marble receiving tomb and Gothic portico; and the new Swan's Building, which was established expressly for the protection of the various birds gracing Lake Hibiscus, a response to the temper of the times, including a harkening back to the early American tradition of journalist-explorer/artist recorder, and a broadening sensitivity to Nature, no less than the manifestation of these ideas flaunted in the pages of such currently popular publications as James J. Audobon's <u>Bird's of America.</u> Although by 1841 Audubon had completed his <u>Birds</u> and watercolors, some of his best watercolors after 1841, an ornithological and naturalist interest continued through his sons, John Woodhouse and Victor Gifford Audubon; (2) the interest in observing and protecting wildlife initiated by their father's work continued to find expression at Forest Hills Cemetery until the present time.

The eighteen-eighties brought a new chapel and office building designed by architects Van Brunt and Howe; the opening of another field, the Field of Heth, following the filling of the Field of Manoah, and new tropical plants, favorites of Victorian America, were laid out thereby rendering Lake Hibiscus increasingly more exotic.

If work in the eighties was completed at a more leisurely pace, work in the nineties, the last decade addressed in this book, began and continued, fast and furious, with large land purchases, the completion of the Field of Heth, the alteration of Lake Dell, and in an act perhaps blasphemous to Dearborn's credo, the cemetery's natural water body was filled-in to allow for the widening of adjoining avenues. Forest Hills Avenue was elongated and received a cobblestone facelift, while more masonry work was done along a rustic wall near Consecration Tomb, the Beech Avenue building, and, near present day Morton Street on a bridge designed by W.G. Preston. The decade of the eighteen-nineties ended on a literary note with the publication of Forest Hills Fiftieth Anniversary Brochure.

Section III:
Overview To The Journal

1. Diane Kelleher. Two volumnes of research notes: <u>KRN:Forest Hills Cemetery, 1979</u>.

2. Theodore E. Stebbins. <u>American Master Drawings and Watercolor.</u> Harper and Rowe (New York: 1971), "Chapter Four: Romanticism in the Early Nineteenth Century", p. 59-84, esp. 78-81.

SECTION IV:

THE HISTORICAL NICHE: THE FOREST HILLS CEMETERY JOURNAL

CHAPTER I:

THE DECADE OF THE FORTIES

1846

ON OCTOBER 5, 1846, the honorable John J. Clarke, Mayor of Roxbury, presented a communication to Roxbury's City Council. He noted that since existing cemeteries were either full or soon to be full, and since Mount Auburn Cemetery was rather far away, what the county needed was a new cemetery. He urged the purchase of land intended for the use of all city inhabitants as a final resting place. He also urged that measures be taken to make existing cemeteries more respectable. The precise text follows:

> GENTLEMEN, - I desire to call your attention to the Burial grounds at the corner of Washington and Eustis Streets and on Warren street. Both of these grounds are in dilapidated condition, and need attention, and at present reflect no honor on the proprietors. The oldest of the two has long been filled, and no bodies are deposited there except in some old family tomb, and the other is nearly filled.

At a time not very remote, it will become necessary to procure other places of sepulture for those that shall die in the city. Mount Auburn is too distant, and but for a comparatively few feel able to procure lots there. I would therefore invite you to consider the expediency of purchasing a tract of land, (if one can be procured well-adapted,) and laying it out in a proper manner, and appropriating it to the purposes of a cemetery for the use of all inhabitants of the city, on such terms and conditions as shall be thought best; and also to take such measures to make the existing cemeteries more respectable. (1)

This communication constitutes the initial impetus which would, some twenty-one months later, culminate in the consecration of Forest Hills Cemetery, Roxbury, Massachusetts, one of America's first rural parks. Clarke's report was referred to a Joint Special Committee, which on November 16, (2) decided in favor of repairing the old cemeteries. In March, the Joint Special Committee Reported that they were unable to find a suitable tract of land, shuffling the matter off to the next city council which was to be formed in thirty days. As planned, the new council convened in April and took up the issue of a new cemetery. There was a difference though. By this time, Henry Dearborn had become mayor. That the issue of a new cemetery would be a persistent one was now guaranteed by The Joint Standing Committee on Burial Grounds with Mayor Dearborn as Chairman. (3).

Throughout the summer, committee members researched available land for the proposed project, most of which was located in Roxbury or what is now West Roxbury, ever mindful that the requisite definition of "suitable" meant: affordable, centrally located, and naturally beautiful. (4) By early Fall, the Committee was able to report that they had indeed found a suitable piece of property, so together with interested citizens, the entire group visited the site and discussed the project. Public sentiment was generally favorable, although some opposition surfaced on financial grounds. Nonetheless, the formal report appeared on September 6, 1847: its enthusiastic author?: Henry Dearborn. The proposed site was Joel Seaverns' Farm, which fronted Canterbury Street, and a small tract of land (7 acres) owned by a Dr. Warren, which was to serve as an entrance avenue. (5)

Dearborn's report was lengthy, beginning with an outline of burial practices of ancient cultures, continuing on to a discussion of Cambridge's Mount Auburn Cemetery, the avenues of which Dearborn had laid out, and finally, to the proposed site and the potential benefits to be derived from the cemetery. The writing is both expository and persuasive; and the significance of the report lay in its publicizing the selected sites, outlining the proposed method of financing, and advocating future purchases. With regard to these issues, it was reported that:

> THE site is Seaverns' Farm, which fronts on Canterbury Street; there is also a small tract of about seven acres that is owned by Dr. Warren, which it is desirable should be obtained, and it is believed ultimately it may be..for the purpose of opening an avenue to Walk Hill Street. The whole farm contains about 85 acres, an outline plan of which, and the adjacent estates in part, accompanies this report for the purpose of presenting the extact position of the land and its subdivisions.

> The Warren lot, with a portion of the tract which includes about 55 acres and is defined in the plan, has been selected for the cemetery. The price

demanded is $350.00 per acre, for the payment of which the notes of the city, redeemable in 10 years and bearing an interest of 6%, will be taken; The Committee therefore recommend that the purchase be immediately made. The remainder of the farm, which contains 30 acres, it is considered by several members of the Committee important to purchase; but as it includes the dwelling house, barns and other edifices, the orchard, garden and the most valuable part of the cultivated land, the price asked is $600.00 per acre; the Committee, therefore, have not been willing to take the responsibility of urging the purchase, but submit the subject to the deliberation and decision of the City Council.

By the annexed statement it will appear that if the cemetery should contain 62 acres, it will form 6,751 burial lots of 300 square feet each, after deducting one quarter of the land for carriage avenues and footpaths. If, then, one fourth the number of lots be sold for $50.00, and the remainder at the average price of $1,000.00, they will produce an income of $590,750. which can be gradually appropriated for the erection of an iron fence, a granite gateway, a chapel, a cottage for the superintendent, and the appropriate and necessary structures, and leave a fund, the interest of which will keep the grounds in the best possible conditions forever.

Although the cost of the land will amount to about $22,000.00, the sale of 440 lots will afford a sum more than sufficient to liquidate the debt incurred in its purchase, and the income from an annual sale of 27 lots will pay the interest.

Should it be considered expedient to purchase the whole farm, the portion which may be appropriated for a cemetery could be better located, if not augmented to advantage, and the entrance to it from Canterbury Street be more conveniently and symmetrically arranged, while the remainder of the land, not included in the cemetery, can be laid out into cottage lots, in such a manner as to render them interesting and valuable as places of residence, from the spacious extent of open grounds in their immediate vicinity, which will be embellished with forest trees, shrubs and flowering plants and thus rendered an important and diversified feature in the surrounding landscape.

Even if the additional land cannot be obtained for less than $60.00 per acre, it is highly probable that in less than 5 years the houselots can be sold for more than double their cost to the city, if the causes that have so remarkably tended to increase the business, population, and resources of Boston and the surrounding towns during the last ten years should continue. Three cents per square foot would amount to over $1300.00 per acre; and it is to be remembered, that all the land in this city must necessarily be enhanced in value, in a ratio equal at least to that of the population, commerce, manufacture, the mechanic arts, and all other branches of industry and trade in the capitol of the State.(6)

(Here we see referenced all of the motives earlier mentioned: pragmatic necessity, civic pride, the development of a park, along with insight into Dearborn's personality, organizational demeanor, business acumen, and visionary demeanor.).

Eventually, all of Seaverns' land would be purchased, although Dearborn's method of financing the cemetery through the sale of residences along the perimeter, an idea recalling the financing of Repton's Regence Park in London, would never materialize, still testimony to England's artistic influence, and urban planning.

Dearborn's plan was to run into opposition, with objections arising predominantly among the Board of Aldermen. "Indeed there was great danger that the project would entirely fail, as there was at first a decided majority against the order adopted by the Common Council...At this juncture, however, a public meeting of citizens in favor of the establishment of a rural cemetery was called and quite fully attended. Addresses were made by General Dearborn and several other gentlemen of taste and influence...and the meeting awakened favorable sentiment." People subscribed for lots and the opposition, which had favored only the establishment of a potter's field, was embarrassed into acquiescence. (7).

Finally, on November, 9, 1847, the following document passed the city council:

> ORDER, for the first purchase of the Seaverns land, passed by both branches of the City Council, November 9, 1847.
>
> Ordered, That the Joint Standing Committee on Burial Grounds be, and they hereby are authorized to purchase of Joel Seaverns, for a Rural Cemetery,

a tract of land called Seaverns Farm, containing 55 acres, more or less, at $350.00 per acre; and the city treasurer is hereby authorized and required to give the note of the city for the amount of the purchase-money of said land, payable in 10 years from the first day of August, A.D. 1847, with interest at the rate of 6% per annum, payable annually.

Ordered, further, That a Joint Special Committee of five be appointed to apply to the General Court, for an amendment to the City Charter, authorizing the City Council to chose Commissioners, or Trustees, not exceeding 5, who shall have the sole care, superintendency, and management of said Cemetery, and report thereon, annually, to the city council; one of whom, after 5 years shall go out of office each year, and one member of said board of Comissioners, or trustees, chosen annually thereafter in the month of April: said amendment to provide further, that a portion of said Cemetery be set apart or appropriated for public burial, free of charge, and also that the proceeds of sales of lots, or rights of burial in said Cemetery, shall be devoted to the liquidation of the debt incurred in the purchase of the land, and to the improvement and embellishment of the Cemetery, under the direction of said Comissioners, or trustees, and that no moneys shall be appropriated from the city treasury by the city council for such improvement and embellishment, together with such other provisions as said committee may deem proper, and for the interest of said Cemetery and of the city. (8).

This purchase order was the first: the future would bring several more.

1848

In accordance with the provisions of the Seaverns' Purchase Order Act, and in accordance with an act signed by the governor on March 24, 1848, 5 Comissioners were chosen by the city council: Mayor Henry Dearborn, Chairman; Alvah Kittredge (the Alderman), Secretary; Henry Codman, George Russell, and an unnamed fifth member, who may well have been Superintendent Brims: and Seaverns' land was officially deeded to the Board of Comissioners. (9)

Henry Dearborn was unanimously chosen as the man to lay out the grounds and he in turn chose Daniel Brims, a Scottish gardener, as his right hand man. Of Brims, it has been said that he was: "a practical man and a man of taste. He from the first showed an appreciation of the ideas and intentions of General Dearborn, and an ability to carry them into effect. Many of the rural embellishments are the results of his taste and skill, and the thoroughness of the work in the construction of avenues and paths, the preparation of the borders and the cultivation of trees, shrubs, and plants are in a great degree attributable to his thorough knowledge of his business, judgment and good taste." (10) In fact, Brims would continue in this capacity as Superintendent many years after Dearborn's death. Intellectual partners: Dearborn designed, Brims implemented.

It was on April 14, 1848, that Dearborn first submitted his plan for laying out the grounds, carriage avenues and paths. (11) Actual work began on April 25, 1848. (12) Dearborn designated ten different parts of the cemetery by name: *Eliot Hills, Fountain Hill, Mount Dearborn, Mount Warren, Consecration Hill, Chapel Hills, Snow Flake Cliff, Clover Hill, Strawberry Hill, Juniper Hill;* including four lakes: *Dell, Woodbine Mere, Lake Hibiscus,* and *Lake Iris,* of which two, Lakes Iris and Hibiscus were scheduled to be excavated. Dearborn advocated the finding, in the near future of an additional water supply, either by forming a reservoir near either the stream west of the cemetery; or the one southeast of Canterbury Street. Further, he proposed that a small steam engine pump water through metallic pipes to Lake Dell from which the water would then be conducted to the remaining three lakes; which would effectively keep the lakes full during the drier months; and provide for aesthetic cascades between Lake Dell and Woodbine Mere and fountains in all the lakes. If all else failed, it was reasoned, Jamaica Pond, later the gemstone of one of Olmstead's crowning achievements, the emerald of Boston's Emerald Necklace, could be tapped and water pumped from there throughout the proposed cemetery. This system, however, would not reach full construction due to financial constraints which later forced the adoption of a variant of Dearborn's initial plan, (13) which still maintained many of its primary characteristics.

Most of the avenues were formed and three hundred to four hundred lots laid out between April and June of 1848. Three miles of carriage avenues and two miles of footpaths were laid out in a manner which provided easy access to all areas and beautiful approaches as well. The avenues are 16 feet wide, the paths 6 feet wide and "defined by lines of sod one foot wide"; and constructed so as to ensure good draining and minimize upkeep. The surfaces of the avenues are convex with gutters on either side to accomodate rainwater runoff; while the road beds are comprised of stone foundations 2 to 3 feet deep atop which is a layer of gravel procured from other areas of the cemetery. (14)

With construction of the avenues and paths well in hand, the time had come to concentrate on the main entrance; but there was a problem: the land. Still, soon forthcoming was: Good News! On May 26, 1848, Dearborn was able to inform the committee that Mr. John Parkinson had agreed to sell twelve acres of land adjoining the property of Joel Seaverns; and that the City Council would soon receive a request for an order to purchase the land.(15) This second land purchase was significant since the affirmative answer from Mr. Parkinson had been prefaced by dishearteningly negative answers from all other land owners in the area. Now the issue was finally settled: Parkinson's land was ready to be used as the landscape foundation for the main entrance. Originally, the Comissioners hoped the main entrance could be located on the southwest side of the cemetery along Walk Hill Street, on land owned by Dr. John Warren, with whom for reasons unknown, the original purchase could not be effected, although Warren was willing to cede a 30 foot wide passageway through his land to Walk Hill Street.(16) The difficulty was, 30 feet was not sufficiently wide for an appropriate entrance, so, in an attempt to remedy the problem, the Commissioners tried to acquire one acre of land to the west of the passageway. This owner, too, declined the terms; the Comissioners were forced to abandon hopes of a main entrance along the southern end of the cemetery and to consider, instead, a second choice: the Northern end. (17). Parkinson's land was along this northwest border and he agreed to sell; so the Parkinson purchase order would pass the city council within the next thirty days on June 26, 1848.

With the purchase completed, Dearborn was ready to submit his plan for the main gateway: the first version of which was brought to fruition sometime in 1848. (18) As expected, it reflected his affinity for the ancients: It was an Egyptian portico, twenty-four feet high and forty-feet wide, with an elegant and elongated frontage one hundred and sixty feet in length. The architectural design prototype was an ancient portico at Garsery located "above the first cataract of the Nile; which had two massive columns, each richly sculptured, and a winged globe on the exterior side of the entablature. Structurally, the portico was secured by a foundation of cedar posts, iron bolts, and stone. Functionally, the forty foot width permitted passage of two horse drawn carriages; from the confines of which were readable, two inscriptions: one passing into the cemetery, "Though I Walk Through the Valley of the Shadow of Death, I Will Fear No Evil"; and another, passing out of the cemetery: "I am the Resurrection and the Life - Consecrated June 28, 1848". (19) (The fact that the gateway was Egyptian, suggests global interest in archeology stimulated by excavations as those at Pompeii, Herculenium and Vesuvius which particularly captivated Europeans, and European-bound American travellers transmitted back to America.).

In 1848, progress was made in several other areas as well. A rustic observatory, 25 feet high and affording view of all of the Blue Hills, parts of the "villages" of Randolph, Milton, Dorchester, Quincy, Jamaica Plain, Brookline, Brighton, Cambridge, Dorchester Bay and several other of its islands, was formed around a large oak tree on the summit of Consecration Hill. (20) Lodges were built on either side of the main gate, one constituting the office of the superintendent (Brims); and one for the gatekeeper; and as was the case with the entrance gate, these two were sanded to resemble Jersey stone. They were connected to the gateway by fences formed of "round pales, over 2 inches in diameter, which are alternately surmounted with lotus blossoms and lance heads; painted allover to resemble bronze." (21) Fences constituted the third highest expenditure, trailing labor costs and interest on Joel Seaverns' property; since six thousand fifteen (6015) feet of fence was erected at a cost of $990.00; much of which was spent on the rustic fence at the southern end of the cemetery. (22)

(Actually, the decision to include various structures tells us a little bit about the society of the time period: the observatory tower, for example, may have been requisite for security reasons: concern for lots with expensive monuments required restrictions to keep potential vandals at bay, and Death's mandate: 'rest in peace' intact. Still, one cannot help but recall the long tradition of panoramic views, engravings, etchings, and chromolithographs of earlier American artists, and especially, the topographical renderings of the port of Boston so long popular with in-town gallery patrons, without acknowledging the environs enamourment with its own geographic reflection. Forest Hills' observatory tower would provide relatively uninterrupted vistas for any artist willing to walk to the top for a clear glimpse of America. Further, such a tower metaphorically continues the ancient odelisk tradition of Europe, as well as America's own traditions *to wit*: the Bunker Hill Monument and the Washington Monument. The rustic fences remind us that we are here temporarily positioned amidst an era enamored with the principles of Jacksonian democracy and hence a cemetery with procured and free public lots; and the legacies of Jeffersonian agrarianism, for the land was, after all, originally surrounded by working farms as included husbandry. Moreover beyond the Transcendentalism of Emerson and Thoreau (Walden) and the Democratic Naturalism of Whitman (Leaves of Grass, Democratic Vistas) echoes of a "Romantic Lyric Naturalism" (our term) seemed to pulsate throughout the century in response to awareness of English poets espousing the glories of God's land, as transcriptions of the beautious European Nature of Wordsworth, Lord Byron and the Lake Poets.)

Lastly, at Forest Hills, lots and graves were prepared for sale and a nursery was begun. Lots and graves in different areas of the cemetery were prepared for sale at various prices: A three-hundred square foot lot could be had for $50.00; and graves (one half to one sixth of a lot) for 16-2/3 cents per square foot; while graves costing five dollars each were to be prepared along the southern side of the cemetery. This latter area was enclosed with a rustic fence and scheduled in the next year to be screened by a buckthorn hedge, divided by footpaths, and embellished with trees and shrubs. On the eastern side of the cemetery was land appropriated for free burials.(23). (With the larger parts of the plan accomplished, the frosting on the cake of Dearborn's Dream began to congeal.)

On a lighter note, the nursery was started, although the exact location remains unknown, with the stipulation that the trees and shrubs were to be used on the grounds, as needed. Dearborn's long-range plan was that "within two years, there will be at least a hundred thousand plants growing therein, from seeds which have been planted, and will be next autumn, of the elm, rock and white maple, beech, ash, chestnut, and mountain ash, hickory, black walnut and other trees." "Orders have also been sent to England for several thousand of the various kinds of forest and ornamental seedling trees of Europe and other countries, from one to three feet high that will flourish in this climate, to plant out in the nursery next spring, as they can be procured for from three to ten dollars per thousand." (24) (Could Dearborn have been anticipating Olmstead's idea of Arnold Arboretum on a smaller scale? Was this an enhancement driven by silent competition with Jacob Bigelow's Mount Auburn? Or the avocative realizations of a visionary dream maker catering to his gentleman farmer past? Or was it an attempt at permanent beautification spurred on by upcoming events?)

On June 9th, the Comissioners met to discuss the Consecration/ Dedication they wished to hold and decided to schedule services for the 28th. In advance of the event, Dearborn formally submitted his list of proposed names for the various lakes, hills, avenues, and paths.(25) These names, parralleling the botanically inspired ones used by Jacob Bigelow, with whom Dearborn had worked at Mount Auburn, were accepted. At a meeting on the 20th, George Russell, in honor of Dearborn's dedication to the Cemetery motioned that the hill bounded by White Oak, Mountain Willow and Red Oak Avenues be named Mount Dearborn. (26) As is customary with dedications, various civic leaders spoke, including, of course, Mayor Dearborn; hymns were sung and prayers offered.(27)

LANDSCAPE ARCHTECTURE DESIGN: DEARBORN'S CEMETERY DESIGNATIONS

<u>Eliot Hills</u>:

Four hills situated between the western bounds of the cemetery and White Oak Avenue, extending north from the gate on Walk Hill Street "to the junction of the northeastern terminus of Eliot Hills path with White Oak Ave." The hills were named for John Eliot, "Teacher" in Roxbury's first church for sixty years beginning in 1632. "He founded the first Indian Protestant Church in North America, in Natick; and such was his holy zeal to civilize the savages, that he translated the whole of the Scriptures into the language of the Natick tribe." He was called "Apostle Eliot".

<u>Fountain Hill</u>:

Bounded on the southwest by Cherry; the southeast by Fountain, the west by Aspen and the north by Willow and Fountain Avenues. Here, a small edifice has been erected to serve as an office. On the northeastern base of this hill there is a natural spring which was enlarged and surrounded with an embankment of rough stone and wild plants. A flat stone was placed over a portion of the spring to preclude the sun's rays from the water. It supports a bronze tablet inscribed: "Whosoever drinketh of this water will thirst again; but the water that he shall give will be in him a well of water springing up into everlasting life." Outside the office is a rough boulder coverd with lichens. On the boulder is a sundial and affixed to the rock is a brass plate with the following eigraph: "*Horzs Non Numero Nisi Serenas*".

<u>Mount Dearborn</u>:

This is bounded by White Oak on the North; Fountain on the East; Willow on the South; and Red Oak Avenue on the West.

<u>Mount Warren</u>: Named after the Revolutionary War general, is defined by Walnut and Tupelo on the North; Rock Maple to the East; White Oak to the South; and the cemetery fence on the western side.

<u>Consecration Hill</u>: Defined by the cemetry fence on the North and East; by Lily Path to the South; and Magnolia and Yew Avenues at the West.

<u>Chapel Hill</u>: Bounded by the cemetery fence, northward; Magnolia and Yew to the East; Chestnut Ave. and the fence, on the South and West. Its name is derived from its proposed function of hosting a chapel.

<u>Snow Flake Cliff</u>: Bounded by Mulberry, to the West; Chestnut and Tupelo northward; Larch to the East; and Walnut Avenue to the South.

<u>Clover Hill</u>: Exists in front of the gate on Canterbury Street between Elm and Beech Avenues.

<u>Strawberry Hill:</u> Bounded by the fence due north; Beech to the West; Elm and Beech to the South.

<u>Juniper Hill:</u> Bounded by the fence, south; and lying between the eastern fence and Fountain Avenue.

DEARBORN'S LANDSCAPE ARCHITECTURE DESIGN: LAKES, AVENUES, AND PATHS

<u>Names of the Lakes:</u>

<u>Woodbine Mere</u>: Southeast of Consecration Hill and north of Lake Iris. (Along with Lake Dell, scheduled to be enlarged and deepened. Lake Iris and Lake Hibiscus may not have been actual lakes in 1848, but rather swampland.)

Lake Dell: Bounded on the North by Consecration and Chapel Hills; by Mount Warren on the South; and by Snowflake Cliff on the West. (It is no longer in existance.)

Lake Iris: East of Rock Maple and North of Elm and Fountain Avenues (probably near present day Cedar).

Lake Hibiscus: South of Elm and East of Fountain (where it is located today).

Names of the Avenues:

Aspen, Beech, Cedar, Cherry, Chestnut, Cyprus, Elm, Fountain, Hemlock, Larch, Liden, Locust, Magnolia, Mount Warren, Mulberry, Red Oak, Rock Maple, Tupelo, Walnut, White Pin, Willow, White Oak, and Yew.

Names of the Paths:

Azalea, Clematis, Clover, Columbine, Cowslip. Elder, Eliot Hills, Fern, Grape, Green Briar, Hawthorn, Hazel Holly, Harebell, Iris, Ivy Kalmia, Lily, Mayflower, Mistletoe, Moss, Primrose Rose, Raspberry, Sumach, Snow-Flake, Strawberry, Sweet Briar, Viburnum, Violet.

*When descriptions of the locations of these avenues are compared with a present day map, twelve coincide totally or closely. One avenue no longer exists. Eleven avenues do not coincide. Part of the difficulty appears to be that Chestnut Avenue, now in the southwest corner of the cemetery, was originally in the northwest corner, near or being synonymous with Consecration Avenue.

The last event of significance occurring during 1848 is expressed in the following order of the city govenment: (29)

SECTION I. The Rural Cemetery recently established by the city council shall be called and known by the name of "Forest Hills".

SECTION II: This ordinance shall take effect from and after its passage.

Passed July 3, 1848.

1849

While the major thrust of activity centered around the preparation of lots for sale and the construction of avenues by which those lots could be reached, additional activity occurred on the entrance, in the nursery, and an architectural undertaking of utmost importance: the receiving tomb.

In order to create more lots, trees with their roots, were removed from footpaths extending between White Oak and Cherry Avenues, from Spin to Fountain Avenue for an aggregate length of 4000 feet. This area, previously covered with a dense grove of trees and shrubs, now afforded 300 new lots. The junctures of the avenues and paths and the ends of the spaces between them were reserved, trenched, bordered with sod or stones, and planted with trees, shrubs, and herbaceous flowering plants to enhance the picturesque features of the grounds, rendering them more diversified, beautiful and interesting. Begun in the previous autumn, the nursery now "claimed special attention". A several thousand seedling forest, and ornamental trees were reared during the year, to be readied for planting in April 1850. New arrivals to the nursery included about 8000 young trees of which there are 14 different varieties including rhododendrons, apparently both rare and much admired in the New England of pre-Civil War America, and of course, there were Kalmias.

The major architectural undertaking of this year was the construction of a receving tomb (which unfortunately is not described in any of the annual reports). Meanwhile, land ceded earlier by Dr. John Warren and located from the southern gate to Walk Hill provided the site for a new entrance; an entranceway more than 500 feet long, and thickly bordered with trees, since it was cut through a natural forest.

Finally, on a business note: during the 18 months since the cemetery opened; 326 lots have been subscribed for, 126 during 1849 alone; 35 of which have been enclosed by iron fences; 31 monuments have been erected; 6 tombs built; and 252 interrments have taken place. (30)

Section IV:

Chapter I: The Decade Of The Eighteen- Forties

1. Text reproduced in W.A. Crafts, <u>Forest Hills Cemetery: Its Establishment, Progress, Scenery, Monuments</u>, Roxbury: John Backup, 1855, Appendix I, p. 173-174.

2. Crafts. <u>Ibid.</u>, p. 174; Forest Hills Cemetery, Annual Report #1, p. 3.

3. <u>Roxbury Municipal Government Report for 1847-48</u>, p. 87, 88.

4. Crafts. <u>Op.cit.</u>, p. 18.

5. Crafts, <u>Ibid.</u>, p. 21.

6. H. Dearborn, "Joint Standing Committee on Burial Grounds Report", September 6, 1847, reproduced in Crafts, <u>Forest Hills Cemetery</u>, p. 187-189.

7.-10. Crafts. <u>Forest Hills Cemetery</u>, p. 27; 193-4; 25; 26; respectively.

11. Board of Comissioners of Forest Hills Cemetery,<u>Annual Report</u>, May 5, 1848.

12. Comissioners, <u>Ibid.</u>

13. Forest Hills Cemetery, <u>Annual Reoprt, No. 1</u>, p. 2; and H. Dearborn, <u>Report</u>, and <u>Minutes</u>, 1848, p. 1-3.

14. Comissioners,<u>Annual Report , 1848</u>; and H. Dearborn, Report, <u>Minutes, 1848</u>, p. 123.

15. Forest Hills Cemetery, <u>Annual Report No. 1</u>, p. 7; and <u>Minutes of Meeting</u>, May 6, 1848.

16. For discussion, see Forest Hills Cemetery, <u>Annual Report No. 1</u>, p. 2.

17. Commissioners, <u>Annual Report No. 1</u>, p. 2.

18. Cemetery, <u>Ibid.</u>, p. 7.

19. Cemetery, <u>Ibid.</u>, p. 8.

20. Cemetery, <u>Ibid.</u>, p. 4, 5, and 6.

21. Cemetery, Ibid., p. 7.

22. Comissioners, , 1848; Forest Hills Cemetery, Annual Report #1, p. 7.

23.-24. Forest Hills Cemetery, Annual Report, No. 1, p. 8.

25. Commissioners, 1848, p. 1,2, 3; See chart in text for details.

26. Comissioners, , 1848, p. 1,2,3.

27. Forest Hills Cemetery, Annual Report for 1898, p. 24. (Fiftieth Anniversary).

28.-29. Forest Hills Cemetery, Ibid.

30. Forest Hills Cemetery, Annual Report, 1849; Comissioners, 1849.

Chapter II

The Decade Of The Fifties:

1850

During the 1850 season, four thousand feet of avenues were completed, which meant that they were trenched, filled up with stones, graveled, defined by sod, and embellished along the borders with trees, shrubs, and herbaceous flowering plants. (1)

The area along the south side of the cemetery, appropriated for single graves, received a name: the Field of Macphelah. (2) (The name, as readers may recognize, was taken from biblical passage: a pattern bound for later repetitions.) As readers may recall, the Field of Macphelah was the "first instance mentioned in the history of the human race of the performance of funeral rites...it was there that Abraham sure of the possession of a burying place for Sarah, his wife, there ... deposited the remains of that patriarch, and of Isaac, Rebekah, and Leah." At Forest Hills, this area was developed due to public interest in response to which two carriage avenues were constructed, one emanating from the south gate and one from the north gate. Several thousand trees were planted between the paths and along borders, and an arbor vitae hedge added along the north and east sides. Access at this time was through an area along the west end of Spruce Avenue through a small iron gate unsupported by granite posts, while a larger gate was planned for that end of Juniper Avenue.

The nursery was again growing: As ten thousand seven-hundred seedlings, sewn from seeds in the Fall of 1848, were transplanted to various parts of the cemetery; sixteen thousand seedling plants, previously imported, were now set out to begin growing in the nursery. The varieties of trees actually planted in various parts of the cemetery at this time included: oak, chestnut, mountain ash, black walnut, white ash, horsechestnut; while the varieties of imported seedlings now in the nursery included: Norway Spruce, Scotch Fir, Sycamore and Linden, imported from England. The varieties of trees whose seeds were sewn in autumn and which would soon be sprouting included: rock maple, mountain or Indian maple, basswood, hop hornbeam, moosewood, beech, mountain ash, sycamore, oaks of several kinds, hickory; some of which species were as novel and unfamiliar to readers then as they are now.(3)

The two final areas of accomplishment for the 1850 season were the avenue from Walk Hill Street to the Cemetery (through Warren's property), and the northern gateway. Along the southern access route (Warren's), trees and shrubs were set out, and a fence erected on the eastern side of the land. The space between Walk Hill and the avenues was filled in, eventually to be enclosed by a rustic fence for the protection of the trees and shrubs to be set out during the next Spring. Two carriage ways, on two sides of the area, would "communicate with the avenue and the street, in such a manner, as to render it convenient and pleasant to pass into or out of the cemetery, through the southern gate."

The northern gateway was scheduled to be improved before vegetation was planted. Improvements consisted of grading the ends of the avenues and paths near the gate, on the interior, and those which connect with Forest Hills Avenue, on the exterior. Further, the general area would receive definition through the sods and stones placed at the border and the eventual planting of trees, shrubs and flowers. (4)

1851

This was the year that West Roxbury was formed. On May 24, 1851, the state legislature passed a bill setting off a portion of Roxbury and incorporating the section under the name West Roxbury. Although Forest Hills Cemetery was located in this section, the legislature provided that the cemetery, along with Brook Farm, would remain under the jurisdiction of Roxbury. Since the cemetery was also to be free from taxation, on June 30, the Roxbury City Council passed an order electing to take the property and assume all liabilities for the cemetery; which was their means of insuring control of the property. We recall Henry Dearborn was Mayor of Roxbury. A similar motivation would, seventeen years later, induce the Comissioners to incorporate, rather than allow the cemetery to become part of Boston, and subject to control by the Boston City Council. (5) Unfortunately, this is the extent of the information available for the 1851 season, since the 1852 annual report has been impossible to ascertain: still the notes do, however, mention an important event: the June 29th death of Henry Dearborn in Portland. He was succeeded as President of the Board of Comissioners by one of its 5 charter members: Alvah Kittredge (6), through whom Dearborn's dreams would continue to grow.

1852

During the fifth year of operation, the popularity of the cemetery as a rural park had grown sufficiently to necessitate the establishment of "a regular omnibus communication...opened to convey persons to and from the grounds." (Unfortunately, Dearborn did not live to see the popularity his cemetery attained as a rural park.). The southern part of the cemetery was planted with a variety of forest trees taken from the nursery, with the area covered amounting to about ten acres. This is also the first year where mention is made of hedges being used (rather than iron) to enclose lots (rather than the boundaries of land parcels). Still, iron work fences remained very popular among those who could afford them. Of the 24 monuments erected, one was of particular interest: General Dearborn's monument, which was erected at the summit of Mount Dearborn.

In the architectural sphere, two large receiving tombs were built, both in the area of Lake Dell, at the juncture of Chestnut and Tupelo Avenues, both 16 feet by 8 feet "and 7 feet high in the clear", both at a cost of $1,000.00. Thus, to date, the completed structures on cemetery property include: the main gateway on Parkinson's land, the observatory, Brims' and the gatekeeper's lodges and various fences.

That 289 private and public interments took place (in the Field of Macphelah) reveal the growing popularity of Forest Hills as a cemetery; which, combined with the popularity, enjoyment and location associated with Lake Hibiscus, precipitated the need to purchase more land. Currently, Lake Hibiscus was both an asset and a liability because it was situated on the border of land owned by Seaverns; a fact which prevented both the lake's extension by excavation in that direction, and the creation of a road encircling the lake, as is in existence today. Throughout the year, the Comissioners had been trying to attain a favorable price on more of Seaverns' land. Early in the Fall, a satisfactory price was agreed upon and the city council voted to purchase the balance of Seaverns' farm: "23 acres 2 qrs. 36 rods, including buildings, for $9,000.00." The purchase of this land filled in the corner of the cemetery so that the boundary was made more regular and complete, also afforded a new source of a large number of potential sods, an expenditure which had been climbing recently and quickly needed to be offset. (7)

The intermingling of politics and cemetery business continued, as the governor and the City Council approved an Act which stated that the city treasurer could invest money given to the Board of Comissioners as grants, bequests, donations, etc., for the establishment of perpetual care with the reservation that this money had to remain separate from the monies of the city treasury, although the city treasurer administered the handling of cemetery money along with the Board of Comissioners, beginning on February 25, 1852. At its inception, and throughout the history of the cemetery, public and private sector interests would benefactorally intermingle as government and cemetery affairs remained intertwined. From the decades of the forties, we recall that early on, Roxbury's Mayor Clarke advocated for the establishment of a cemetery; that it was after architect Dearborn became mayor that the cemetery was actually established and its committees made permanent. To facilitate funding, the city government willingly issued notes to the cemetery for land purchases, with the stipulation that certain Roxbury residents, the poor and the indigent, receive consideration expressed in terms of gratuitous interment. The council chose the cemetery Commissioners in 1848; shielded the cemetery from the effects of redistricting in 1851; arranged for the cemetery to remain free from taxation; and later, for the City Council to assume all liabilities including those for perpetual care. With this latter provision was culminated the seriated interventions, both the rights of subscription to Forest Hills as a cemetery, and the rights of enjoyment of Forest Hills as a rural park. During the next decade, in response to the Civil War, the city government would bear the cost of a granite fence around the Soldier's Lot, in memorium of Roxbury's fallen soldiers.

1853

It was also decided that the small tool shed, erected at the commencement of operations at the cemetery was "insufficient for present purposes" and that the land under it would be better utilized for lots. Meanwhile, "The Commissioners, last summer, caused the barn, 24 x 22 feet, and the shed, 21 x 17 feet, which were situated on land last purchased of Joel Seaverns, to be removed to a more central location; and had the same put in good order for the safe keeping of tools, for the storage of cement... This year marks the death of another Comissioner, Henry Codman, who before his death on November 4, 1853, had twice been elected to serve as a Comissioner. The annual report states: "In announcing this event, we are reminded of his attention to the duties in the early laying out of the Cemetery.", and reminded that the "name of Forest Hills was adopted by his suggestion." Jonathan French succeeded him as Acting Comissioner until he was formally elected in 1854. Improvements in the cemetery included the grading of Forest Hills Avenue, so that the ascent to Dearborn's Egyptian gateway was made easier and more pleasant. Lake Hibiscus was enlarged and improved by excavations to the south side so as to better incorporate Spring Island, which was formed in the lake, near the northwestern border. The island, so named because of a natural gushing spring around the top of it, which discharges three gallons of water per minute even in the drier months of summer was of great importance to the Cemetery particularly on account of the purity of the water and its central location in the grounds where so many workmen are occupied." The loam removed during excavation was used in preparing lots and borders, and cultivating grass, flowers and shrubs. Spring Island was the first manmade island; a second,

Swan Island, would follow. (9). (In some senses, it was left to others to complete some of the most interesting developmental aspects of the cemetery, after Dearborn's vision and politics set the ball rolling.)

During this year was constructed a convenient retreat for visitors in the event of sudden showers and storms."(10) The idea of a visitor's building reappears in later years.

1854

The activities for this year are comparatively less than in previous ones. The main operations included the construction of avenues (1, 540 feet) and paths (1,500) feet; that is, the loam atop them was removed and they were relayed with stone and gravel. During the summer, Lake Hibiscus was enlarged by 20,000 square feet to allow for construction of a second island, Swan Island, 240 feet in circumference with a substantial wall around it. Author, Augustus Crafts tells us this island was built specifically for the use by the swans, (11) hence its name. This deferential treatment of various botanical, ornithological, and wildlife species, characteristic of the nineteenth century, reflected broader cultural concerns which included a respect for divinely created living creatures characteristic of an ontologically conceived society; which was in turn, again philosophically bifurcated by the Empiricists, such as Naturalists like Audubon, Darwin, and Thoreau; and the followers of a type of cosmological mysticism, well-exemplified by the otherworldly Romanticism of painters such as Thomas Cole ("The Voyage of Life") or Washington Allston ("Moonlit Landscape") or Albert Pinkham Ryder ("Toilers at Sea") as science and spirit comingled.

At the cemetery, progress in the structural sphere included the addition of a blacksmith's shop and the removal of a barn and shed. The blacksmith's shop was erected on the most southerly corner of the cemetery grounds, near Canterbury Street; and apparently necessitated because prior to its existence, the cemetery had to send its "drills and picks quite a distance for sharpening; an inconvenience the shop, erected at a cost of about $80.00, readily resolved". Removal of the barn and shed, begun in 1853, was accomplished at a cost of $314.00; thus the expenditures for the year reveal L & D. A. Hodgdon as responsible for moving the shed and the barn, both; and constructing the blacksmith's shop. It is unclear to what extent, if any, wrought iron was forged in the new blacksmith's shop. We do know that the cemetery was embellished with living ornamentation: arboreal enhancements, because of payment notations to S. H. Hatch for roses, shrubs, and plants, and entries for tree payment made to S. Walker and Alvah Kittredge. (12)

1855

Work on Lake Hibiscus spilled over from the previous year, as again, the focus was on enlarging its surface area, this time by 16,000 square feet; and constructing a wall encircling the newly excavated portion, and grading and sodding the border out to the avenue. By now, Lake Hibiscus had acquired such a reputation as a scenic treasure, that it was the increase in the number of visitors which necessitated the widening of the avenues on both the west and north sides, by four feet, from 16-20, thus facilitating both pedestrian and carriage traffic. With more lots needed, the nursery was moved to the southern portion of the yard; and only one expenditure: one purchase, was made: a gravel hill of about 2 acres owned by the City of Roxbury and located along Bourne Street.(13)

1856

Avenue and path construction proceeded as usual: 1600 feet of avenues, 850 feet of paths. At Lake Hibiscus, to prevent the possibility of accident, a fence consisting of stone posts connected by straight iron bars, was constructed on the south side.

A new area was designed for graves: the Field of Ephron, which occurred when it became apparent that the Field of Macphelah was rapidly becoming full. The new area was located in the northern part of the cemetery near Snow-Flake Cliff and today's office, and as with its predecessor, derived its name from Biblical passage. The Field of Ephron is mentioned in Genesis 23:17. In the sixties another section would be called the Field of Manoah; in the nineties, the Field of Heth would be created,

To date, the total grounds of Forest Hills has reached "104 acres, 1 quarter and 6 rods"; the total cost of the land: $36,894.67. According to the minutes, this was also the year when Superintendent Brims threatened, but then withdrew, his resignation: at this time, no explanation was given.(14)

1857

Work on the avenues and paths was in advance of that of previous years: 2,000 feet of avenues and 955 feet of paths received attention. But it was the new Field of Ephron which required the lion's share of man-hours. First, the old wall, on the northwest side, was removed, and a fence corresponding in style with the other parts of the Cemetery was built. Then the avenue, made in part during the previous season, was extended in a relatively circular route so as to terminte at its entrance on Mulberry Avenue, near the Egyptian gateway. (This was Chapel Avenue according to an 1898 map.) "To accomplish this work it was necessary to cut through a large rock a distance of 75 feet, and the whole is now completed. The stone thus removed in grading the avenue was found very convenient, but a few yards distant, in constructing the paths between the ranges of graves; the item of greatest expense in the opening of the avenues, becoming thus a matter of economy in the grading of the paths."(15)

Sometime this year the Boston Fire Department's Cemetery Association purchased a large, beautifully situated lot on Cypress Hill, located between Cypress and Poplar Avenues, readied for next Spring and according to period guidebooks, just as quickly one of the modern day cemetery's attractions, along with Lake Hibiscus.

Mr. Brims, having considered resignation the previous year, did so in actuality, due to the state of his health.

Finally, the annual report for 1857 describes the following event:

> While the men employed upon the avenue which encircles the summit of Consecration Hill were removing loam near the top of the hill, about 4 feet from the surface of the ground, they came upon two human skeletons, or, more properly, upon the bones of 2 once human beings. The 2 sets of bones were lying side by side, separated only by a few inches from each other. They seemed to have been packed in wood ashes, a large quantity being found with the bones. In the opinion of a physician, who was present soon after exhumation, the bones were those of a male and female; and a quantity of long black hair, in a matted state, found at the head of one set of these bones, indicated that it had once covered and adorned the head of a female. These bones of the unknown dead were suitably cared for by our Superintendent, who had them buried in a grave in the Field of Ephron; and it is the intention of the Commissioners to procure a slab, with a suitable inscription, to mark the spot where they are deposited. It is a matter of reasonable conjecture, however, that as this hill was a part of the land which many years ago was owned by the town of Roxbury, and as it was formerly customary in this place to remove persons visited with small-pox from their families and from the neighborhood of human

habitations, it is possible that the top of this hill may have been the site of some rude hospital for the reception of those suffering under this disease.(16)

1858

In March, Oliver Moulton was appointed Superintendent. He began his activities in April, and on the first day of May, Mr. Brims left for Canada. The horses and carts owned by Brims were bought for the cemetery; and a barn on the premises was "fitted up for the reception of the horses, at a cost of $427.05." A cottage, built near the main entrance to the cemetery for occupation by the new Superintendent, and which also contained a room for the uses of persons visiting the Cemetery, was constructed by Kendall and Wood, at a cost of $3,867.02, sometime between June and November.(17) The minutes also reveal that repairs were made to Seaverns' house and that two additional tenements were to be constructed; while the fixing of the shed attached to the house was an activity left to Mr. Head.

Expenditures denote drafts made to E. Augustus Story for trees; this is Judge Story; some of whose trees doubtless lined the 1,000 feet of avenues and 2200 feet of paths constructed during this year.

1859

Avenues? 800 feet...Paths? 1500 feet.

Lots? Twenty seven enclosed with iron fences, 5 with hedges, and 4 with granite curbing: the first instance of granite curbing since for now, iron fences continue to be popular, as the choice of the "well-heeled".

Kittredge and Head were appointed to a committee to take the necessary measures regarding the purchase of the estate of the heirs of Frederick Chandler in November. The annual report tells us that a lot of land, containing 36,250 square feet, purchased from the heirs of Frederick Chandler; (18) located on Canterbury Street, bounded on the remaining the sides by cemetery property and consisting of a house and land, constituted one of the larger expenditures: $750.00.

Finally, a drain was deepened through land of John Parkinson, in order to both facilitate better drainage and to ease the draining of water from Lake Hibiscus, should further excavations enlarging the lake be required or desired, which of course, they would be.

Section IV:
Chapter II: The Decade Of The Fifties

1.   Forest Hills Cemetery,.Meeting Minutes 1850.

2.   Augustus Crafts, Forest Hills Cemetery, p 98; Cemetery,'.Meeting Minutes 1850.

3.   Commissioners, Annual Report, 1850.

4.   Cemetery,.Meeting Minutes 1850.

5.   Roxbury City Document #1, Mayoral Address, January 1852, p. 11.

6.   Cemetery,.Meeting Minutes, May 20, 1852, p. 10.

7.   Commissioners, Forest Hills Cemetery Annual Report, 1953.

8.   Cemeterys,.Meeting Minutes, May 20, 1953, p. 10.

9.   Crafts, Forest Hills Cemetery, p. 98.

10.   Commissioners, Annual Report, 1853.

11.   Crafts, Op.cit., p. 98.

12.   Cemetery, Meeting Minutes, 1854; Commissioners, Annual Report, 1853.

13.   Cemetery, Meeting Minutes 1855; Commissioners, Annual Report, 1855.

14.   Commissioners, Annual Report, 1856.

15.   Commissioners, Annual Report, No. 10, p. 83; Cemetery, Meeting Minutes 1856.

16.   Commissioners, Annual Report, 1857.

17.   Cemetery, Meeting Minutes, June 18, 1858, p. 19.

18.   Cemetery, Meeting Minutes, November 4, 1859, p. 22.

Chapter III

The Decade Of The Sixties

1860

Lake Hibiscus continued to undergo excavation: one and one half acres were excavated to a depth of five feet, so that, at present, three and one quarter acres constitute the water surface area, with another three fourths of an acre scheduled to be excavated. (1) Apart from the continued work on Lake Hibiscus, four areas warranted attention; the completion of a greenhouse; a land purchase effected with Edmund M. Fowler; the erection of General Sumner's monument; and notations referring to the use of granite borders. The greenhouse, apparently begun in the preceding year, and completed during this year, was 70 feet in length; "divided for a propagating house", so as to afford the cemetery the financial advantage of preparing its own plants: and designed by "G. Evers", listed among expenditures as "Plan for greenhouse - $15.00."(2) There was, however, no listing for any type of vegetation for seeds for the greenhouse, among the expenditures.

The Fowler land deal, a 22 acre parcel which borders on Walk Hill and Canterbury Streets in West Roxbury, was well-negotiated for

$9,000. The purchase of this parcel, important since it offers space for extending present avenues, was recommended on November 2, and by December 1, the city had issued a script. (3)

A monument honoring General Sumner was erected on Sumner's Hill. The work, created by N. Cantala Papotti of Rome, was of marble and granite with a platform of 3 steps sustaining the pedestal and statue. The first step was of Quincy Marble, the next two of Italian white marble. Life-sized, the kneeling figure represented the angel of the Tomb protecting the ashes of the dead; while the poppy buds adorning the angel's head were symbolic of eternal sleep; and the urn, the repository of the deceased. (4) Sumner's monument is an appropriately instructive place to pause to refresh our memory of the intent of cemeteries and their sculpture since this monument reflects many *a propos* issues. As a sepulchral monument, Papotti's statue of Sumner awakens memories of the deceased general, softening the grieving process; while it is aesthetically enlightening as it offers a glimpse of an elegant statuary form amidst a Transcendentalist location: Nature, thus calling to mind also a reverence for divinity in Nature. Conservatives would have admired the work and its location at Forest Hills. Situated in a rural park, this monument serves multiple masters: while based on the thoughts, achievements and memories of an actual military man, the monument revers the process of Death, while celebrating and glorifying such national values as civic pride and American patriotism, as history, government, reformism, aesthetics, and reverence merge in this outdoor statuary pavilion.

Until fairy recently, enclosures have been fairly faithfully accomplished in ironwork, hedges, or some type of stone; but this year, nine were completed and composed of hand hewn granite, a new type of stone presentation which added much to the attractiveness of the cemetery, especially on lots at the corner of converging avenues.

Finally, we see that in the cemetery documentation, there were three other interesting notations: one amidst the expenditures, one in the meeting minutes, the third pertaining to the avenues. Expenditures reveal payment of $186.23 made to A.G. Day for "labor and materials on the Chandler house", indicating renovation. The minutes mention that on September 26, Kittredge was authorized to sign a petition against paying taxes to the city of Roxbury. And, lastly we note that avenue and path development proceeded at a healthy pace: 1200 feet of avenues and 1400 feet of paths reached completion within the past twelve months. (5)

1861

At last, the four acres of Lake Hibiscus have been excavated. The annual report states, the lake is finished; but naturally, it was not finished, as later, embellishments would continue to be made. But, for now, the drain from the lake, which was excavated about 700 feet in length through the land of A. J. Peters, was walled: three feet high, which was intended to "give permanence to an important outlet of the surplus water". (6)

On September 23, Kittredge signed another tax protest. Later, the debate with the city Selectmen was settled: the $52.16 the cemetery paid as tax assessment on the cottage was refunded; (7) and correctly so, as we recall from an earlier discussion of politics and business, that the cemetery was exempt from taxes so long as it maintained a section for public burials.

Regarding lot enclosures, this marks the first year where no hedges were used, in addition to which, there was also a marked increase in the use of granite borders. Path excavation amounted to 2,335 feet; while there were no excavations of avenues for the first time since the opening of the cemetery.(8) Lastly, the expenditures list reveals drafts to J. Beck and Son, for flower seed, and D. Welch, the gardener, for bulbs, perhaps indicating the everyday use of the greenhouse.(9)

1862

Resumption of avenue excavation yielded 1700 feet of new walking space, as path work continued and lots were enclosed with iron, granite, and hedges. Meanwhile, the September 5 meeting minutes tell us that Mr. Head built an addition to the rear of the shed at the stable; Kendall and Wood placed the barn on the old Fowler property; and before Thanksgiving, Commissioner Lewis executed plans for the Soldier's Lot.(10) The Commisioners began investing in U. S. Bonds; rather than expending money: "in view of a large expenditure in the renewal of the present gateway in granite; and the inlaying of permanent walls where the cemetery is bounded by the highway." The last entry, a financial one, lists: J.D. Steele, scrip for lot, $10,000.00."(11)

1863

Choosing a design and architect for a new main gateway to replace Dearborn's wooden one was the year's most pressing event. It seems several commissioners had a hand in this undertaking. A two-member board of Lewis and Bumstead was elected from among the Commissioners in March to procure plans for a main entrance gateway and flanking fence. (12) Five months later, another commitee composed of Alvah Kittredge and Lewis was given the responsibility of choosing an architect to review the gateway models already submitted. On August 18, Gridley Bryant, upon review of all the models, announced the Committee's preference - Charles' Panters' design. (13). Panters, a Brookline architect had submitted a model of a Gothic style gateway, which is in place today. It was elegant for the time and the place, when it was proposed. Early in October, Panter, accompanied by Bryant and Sturgis, visited Emanuel Church to review the stonework; the importance of which lies in the scrutiny of materials chosen, since Alexander Esty's Emanuel Church, built two years earlier in 1861 in Boston's Back Bay, was an important model and prototype in the use of Roxbury puddingstone. (14) With the viewing completed, the decision was finalized: the new gateway would be made of Roxbury puddingstone, and work on Panters' gateway would begin in the summer of 1864.(15) Thus, art historically, the focus had now shifted away from marble and granite and Europe, toward embracing native materials; if not in the style of the gateway, at least in the local materials adopted; to effect a compatible merger of the old and the new, of the foreign and the indigenous. Meanwhile, within the gates of the cemetery, 1450 feet of avenues were excavated; the area on Chestnut Hills Avenue at the gateway was improved to facilitate access, and the grade on Mulberry Avenue was lowered and widened for the same reason.

1864

Lake Dell, located between Tupelo and Chestnut Avenues near the main gateway, was deepened; and a granite capped wall constructed so as to encircle the excavated periphery. Resources were so delegated that masonry work could continue beautifying another acre of the cemetery as well, that being: Mount Warren. Bordering along its south side, a wall was fashioned 605 feet in length, 3 feet deep and, including the foundation 9-1/2 feet high - indeed an impressive undertaking by any standards. Thus, it is not surprising that masonry work formed a substantial part of the annual budget, since the estimate for work on Lake Dell was in the vicinity of $12,000; a significant outlay, since as we will learn later,

Lake Dell, as an acquatic attraction, was short lived. In the end, it was filled in completely. (17)

The Soldier's Lot received special attention: the foundation was laid, and the massive granite fence surrounding it was set and leaded, the cost of which was born by the city government. (18) To soften the lot's appearance, banks around it which circumscribe the periphery were softly graded. As it stood, the Soldier's Lot subscribed to general expectations that lots being smaller, more compactly organized, more readily lent to enclosure, than their more expansive counterparts, the fields.

In August, eight years after its opening, the Field of Ephron was closed. (19) Consequently, the Field of Manoah in the southern part of the cemetery was laid out for purchasers of single graves; an expensive proposition since, for topographical reasons, extensive under-drains, 1220 feet of them in fact, were laid in this area. Still more land would be necessitated and eventually available with the Commissioners' purchase of 6 acres of land, the Warren Lot, from J. Sullivan Warren. This parcel was bounded westerly by Walk Hill Street and on all other sides by cemetery property. Just as the Seaverns' land purchase of 1852 had helped to regularize the easterly border of cemetery property, so too, along its Canterbury Street border was the overall westerly line straightened with the Warren purchase. This line would be further extended in the 1870s. (20)

Of the materials employed to enclose individual lots, granite was still the more consistently favored: 17 lots were demarcated by this type of stone, while 2 iron fences were added; and 2 removed; which constituted the first instance of removal of iron fences from lots. While the specific reason for the removal of these fences was unannounced at the time, leaving us to posit rust, difficulty of upkeep on lots without perpetual care, or wartime uses for iron, since the trend away from iron towards granite enclosures roughly coincides with the Civil War years - the Meeting Minutes of 1884 reveal still another explanation of this change of sentiment.

1865

The events of this year were marked by both personal sadness and artistic achievement. On January 26, Commissioner William J. Reynolds who had been an early advocate of the cemetery and a long-time enthusiast and who had served on the Board for 13 years: died. Nine months later, Commissioner Francis C. Head died. Head, author of several annual reports, was also an early friend of the cemetery. He was elected to the first board and served thereafter for 17-1/2 years. "He was particularly instrumental in procuring the present site."

On a happier note, a Norway Spruce hedge was set out on 2 sides of the Field of Manoah and for the first time paving of rain gutters, 1380 feet, is mentioned.(21)

Forest Hills Avenue received its share of attention due to construction of the new gateway. Trees were removed from in front of the cottage to provide good views for the gate, and in April, the first stones were laid for the new gateway. On July 10th, the Commissioners' Reports and random newspapers of local interest noted the event. By the Fall, all that remained to be done on the gateway were minor points which would be accomplished in warmer weather. In addition to architect Panter, the persons responsible for the gate included: Edward Meany of Boston (creator of wrought iron dressings, and ornamental mouldings of freestone from New Brunswick's Caledonia Quarries); Timothy McCarty (supplier of rubblestone); and Michael Killian (the master mason). The Commisioners described the gateway as predominantly "modern Gothic", "very happy in architectural effect and purity of detail", which with its combination of free-stone mouldings and rectangular rubblestone walls, was considered "picturesque and harmonious, and illustrating a style of construction somewhat peculiar to this section, at least, of the country," and hence, unique. The gateway, chosen from among 11 designs (the architects of which are unknown) was described as follows:

> An archway for carriages in the center, of ample width and beautiful proportions, is flanked by 2 towers, square at the base and changing to an octagon at the cornice line of the two flanks or lodges of the Gateway: which are connected with the towers by curtains, in which on either side is an archway for pedestrians. The curtain, between the towers, and connected with these, has a trefoiled arcade, over which the curtain finishes in a crocketted gablet, and the two towers become pinnacles of delicate proportions, as the crowning features of the whole composition.(22)

From the business office, commissioners write that the greenhouse was doing well: almost $300.00 worth of flowers were sold by McLaren, the gardener; while expenditures reveal a draft to George L.D. Barton for "Views of Old Gateway", which would have been Dearborn's original design, for almost $100.00 (23)

1866

During this year, lodges flanking the main gate were finished; and the space around the gate flagged with North River stone; while massive iron stages were forged by Warren Truck and Company according to Panter's Designs. Of the work begun on a fence to enclose the total area of the cemetery; 100 feet, beginning at the northwest lodge, was completed; the design and materials coinciding nicely with the main gate.

In addition, three land purchases were made: The first, was of three acres, possibly purchased from Ann Seaverns and located on Canterbury Street opposite the south end of the cemetery near the contemplated gateway. "The object of this purchases was to secure a site for the buildings now standing on cemetery grounds: so that land under the buildings could be used for lots". The second purchase, effected in September, was 21 acres of A. J. Peters' land bounded to the west by the cemetery; to the north by Forest Hills Avenue "as a guarantee that unsightly constructs would not devalue lot holder's property". The third purchase was 2-1/2 acres of Isaac M. Cary, located on the northwest side of Forest Hills Avenue, purchased to further insure control of the road; and which was no less than 75 feet wide all the way around at any point.

Generally, 1700 feet of avenues and 400 feet of paths were completed, 6 iron fences were removed, a new type of tomb (a wrought granite front style) was constructed for C. W. Cartwright. (24)

1867

Forest Hills Avenue was thoroughly regraded to present a more graceful approach and appearance. Edgestones were set on the north and northwest sides. As in the previous year, three land purchases were transacted; involving H. D. Williams (17,251 feet) on the west side of Forest Hills Avenue to facilitate beautification of the avenue; from I Cary (150) for the same purpose of extending the plant conservatory and enhancing propagation.),

Generally, 1400 feet of paths and 60 feet of avenues were prepared, eight iron fences were removed from lots; and amidst the expenditures list; Swain and Craft were paid for "grape seed", and Michael Cary for "whippletree". (25)

1868

H. D. Williams, a land abutter, allowed the Commissioners to move his wall back far enough to widen Forest Hills Avenue; then promptly donated the land. In addition to this donation, purchase took place as well; two transactions, in fact, one negotiated for 5-1/2 acres from George Simmons along Bourne Street, purchased to secure sand and gravel; the second, 2760 feet from I. Cary along Union Terrace which was to provide better frontage for the double tenement.

As in the late forties and early fifties; in the sixties, politics would play a part in cemetery events. Now, the Board of Commissioners became the Board of Trustees and Forest Hills formally incorporated rather than risk being managed by the city of Boston after Roxbury's annexation to Boston.

The greenhouse (or more properly: the conservatory) was moved from the central part of the cemetery and the material used to build a larger conservatory located at the northerly corner of the cemetery near the gate and the Superintendent's cottage. Meanwhile, 2 propagating houses:(2 having dimensions of 100 feet by 12 feet, and the centrally located one, 100 by 16 feet) were erected, parallel to each; both heated by hot water. The conservatory contains a potting room at the north end; and a reservoir, located underneath the building, capable of holding 54,000 gallons of fluid and measuring 36 feet by 325 feet, at all points, 8 feet deep. Its water is amassed and stored, having been conducted from rain gutters atop several buildings.

Near the conservatory, on Union Terrace, a double tenement house was built for the Assistant Superintendent and the gardener, while the Superintendent's Cottage was enlarged by one room to accommodate his family. On a general note, an iron fence was started along the periphery of the grounds; as was a 60 foot wall extending from the main gate, to form an egress for funeral trains. (26)

1869

Activity centered around Forest Hills Avenue, the erecting of two new buildings, and fences. Forest Hills Avenue, regraded from Morton Street, another gateway, also had the flanking gutters paved, and edgestones set along the South side; while the border between the cemetery wall and the avenue was seeded. On the opposite side, a walk 10 feet wide was covered with concrete.

An iron wall was put in along the South side of the cemetery and a 7 foot tall temporary picket fence erected around most of the rest of the cemetery. To accommodate the Trustees' horses, a stable was built near the Superintendent's Cottage on Union Street, and a blacksmith's shop moved from the cemetery grounds on Canterbury opposite the cemetery (on land purchased in 1866.) (27)

Section IV: Chapter III:
The Decade Of The Eighteen-sixties

1. Forest Hills Cemetery, Board of Commissioners, <u>Annual Report, 1860</u>.

2. Forest Hills Cemetery, <u>Ibid.</u>

3. Forest Hills Cemetery, <u>Meeting Minutes</u>, Fowler Purchase Order, November 20, 1860.

4. Ibid., <u>Meeting Minutes</u>, September 26, 1860.

5. <u>Ibid.</u>, September 26, 1860.

6. Commissioners, <u>Annual Report, 1861</u>.

7. Cemetery, <u>Meeting Minutes</u>, September 23, 1861, p. 26.

8. Commissioners, <u>Annual Report, 1861</u>.

9. Ibid. Cemetery, <u>Meeting Minutes, 1861</u>.

10. Cemetery, <u>Meeting Minutes</u>, prior to November 25, 1862.

11. Commissioners, <u>Annual Report, 1862</u>; Cemetery , <u>Meeting Minutes, 1862</u>.

12. Cemetery, <u>Meeting Minutes</u>, March 30, 1863, p. 33.

13. <u>Ibid.</u>, August 18, 1863, p. 35.

14. Cemetery, <u>Meeting Minutes</u>, October 17, 1863, p. 35.

15. Cemetery, <u>Meeting Minutes, 1863</u>

16. Ibid. Commissioners, <u>Annual Report, 1863</u>.

17. Commissioners, <u>Annual Report, 1864</u>; and Forest Hills Cemetery, <u>Meeting Minutes, 1864</u>.

18. Cemetery, <u>Meeting Minutes, 1864</u>.

19. Cemetery, <u>Meeting Minutes</u>, August 16, 1864.

20.   Commissioners, <u>Annual Report, 1864</u>; Cemetery, <u>Meeting Minutes, 1864</u>; and Purchase Order.

21.   Commissioners, <u>Annual Report, 1865</u>, p. 47.

22.   Commissioners, <u>Annual Report, 1865</u>, Cemetery, <u>Meeting Minutes, 1865</u>.

23.   <u>Ibid.</u>

24.   Commissioners, <u>Annual Report</u>; Cemetery, <u>Meeting Minutes, 1866</u>; and Purchase Orders for I. Carey and A.J. Peters properties.

25.   Commissioners, <u>Annual Report</u> <u>1867</u>; Cemetery, <u>Meeting Minutes, 1867</u> and Purchase Orders for Williams and I. Carey properties.

26.   Commissioners, <u>Annual Report, 1868</u>; Cemetery, <u>Meeting Minutes, 1868</u>; and Purchase Orders for P.A. Simons and I. Carey.

27.   Commissioners, <u>Annual Report, 1869</u>; Cemetery, <u>Meeting Minutes, 1869</u>.

CHAPTER IV

THE DECADE OF THE SEVENTIES

1870

In 1870, activities entailed land acquisition, the building of a new Receiving Tomb, lot maintenance, and the completion of the fence around the periphery; work on which had been delayed due to activities along the Canterbury Street gravel bank. Throughout the cemetery, 2,000 feet of avenues, 1500 feet of paths were excavated, and the number of interments in this initial year of the new decade numbered 746.

The Field of Manoah, nearly full, was extended significantly with the addition to the field of a segment three times as large as the original, and affording 3,000 new graves; for which underdrains were constructed and the avenues, originally on two sides of the old field, were extended and made to circumscribe the field in its entirety.

During the summer of 1870, the trustees bought 18 acres 2 quarters, 9,105 feet of land from Jacob Seaverns along the northern border of the cemetery; the purchase of which gave the cemetery's north line a perfectly straight route extending from Walk Hill Street to near the northeast end of the cemetery. Including this parcel; the present total acreage of the cemetery grew to 175 acres, approximately three-fourths again its size in 1856, at which time it comprised 105 acres. Upon review of the expenditures, we note an unexplained "Purchase of lot, $350.00"; "House and land, Canterbury Street, $1,400.00; and Jacob Seaverns' property, $18,70.00".

Excluding the Seaverns' land acquisition, the highest financial outlay of the year was for a new Receiving Tomb, $10,617.73; one at once larger, of a different construction than the previous tomb, and necessitated, due to the lack of space. Apparently, so many coffins had backed up during the winter, that often as many as 15 had to be removed in the Spring before the appropriate one was located for burial. Initially, in consideration of the projected plan, the trustees visited the Rural Cemetery at Troy, New York, the Albany Cemetery and the Greenwood Cemetery, Brooklyn, New York to review their receiving tombs, hoping to find a proper design.

These trips proved unsuccessful. As a consequence, the Trustees elected a Committee to oversee construction of a tomb and choose architects. The architects chosen were Emerson and Fehmer from the prestigious Boston firm by that name. The selected site: the side of a hill, east of the old tomb, near Lake Dell. Work underway, the superintendent and the cemetery men did blasting; James Pottle of Fairhaven Marble and Marbleized Slate Company supplied the catacomb's slate and marble; and John Leighton built up the tomb. The new tomb contained 286 catacombs; was 75 feet 9 inches long; 37 feet deep; and constructed in the shape of a "T". The catacombs themselves, were 5 tiers deep, arranged on each side of the arched passages, which were 10 feet wide and 10-1/2 feet high, and paved with black and white marble tiles. Three circular shifts extended from the ceiling up to the top of the ground covering the tomb, providing light and air. The catacombs themselves were numbered, and drains provided, such that each could be washed as necessary. While the outside walls, inside partitions and arches were brick, laid in cement, the catacombs were faced with Vermont Slate, and given white marble doors with strong, composition bronze handles. The architect's design included extra large catacombs and all clamps were copper rather than iron, partly for reasons of aesthetics, but also no doubt to decrease acceleration of rusting. (1)

1871

The Field of Manoah, the portico for the new Receiving Tomb, and land acquisition were, again, the major concerns of this year. The Field of Manoah, having been in existence several years, received a border of Norway Spruce planted along its new section, according with the border along the old section.

But, more importantly, the new Receiving Tomb portico was completed; the old tomb was removed, land graded and the avenue widened. The portico itself was designed by Emerson and Fehmer to form the vestibule at the entrance to the tomb. It was 28 feet 8 inches square, built of white Concord granite, in Gothic style; and while the arches of the external walls opened onto the portico; the rear wall, functionally, opened into the tomb. The exterior arches, columns, buttresses, gables and finials were all "relieved by judicious use of foliated ornament", characteristic of Gothic embellishment; while the roof was covered with diverse patterns in red slate; the 'flat ' above with copper, and the whole surmounted with a cresting of ornamental ironwork. On the inside the beams and ceilings were finished in oak; while the arched doorway, from the portico to the vaults, contained gates of open ironwork, on either side of which was room for mural tablets or inscriptions. This year, the total expenditures of the Receiving Tomb, totaled almost $33,000.00.

Other important purchases for 1871 included: 37 acres, 2 quarters, 6919 feet on the south side of Canterbury Street, from the heirs of Betsey Williams; and of the Honorable A.Q. Austin (for sods); and 87,679 feet of land near the gateway, again from I. Carey, and again effected so as to maintain control over Forest Hills Avenue. Thus, total real estate expenditures ran close to $19,000.00.

1872

A less ambitious year than the preceding one, during 1872, work was oriented toward the Receiving Tomb, the grading of nearby grounds as part of the finishing process; while new architectural developments progressed steadily on the construction of a "Swan Building", 28 feet by 12 feet, for the protection of the birds, during the winter months, which in recent years, had become severe enough to damage and destroy hedges on several lots. Avenue and path construction continued at the usual rate, common in preceding years. (3)

1873

If 1872 was a lean year for building, 1873 was the opposite. Numerous structures came into existence within the intervening twelve months. First, a new stable, 80 feet by 40 feet was constructed on the south side of Canterbury Street since the old one, acquired with the land 21 years before was inconveniently located and lacking enough room for hay storage. The stalls in the new structure were along the south side basement area, which is two feet higher than the yard into which they open, conveniently under which is located a hidden manure cellar. Including paddocks, the stable areas bordered 135 feet along the street; simultaneously set back 165 feet; on the east and south sides of which are sheds, constructed for storing wagons and other necessary equestrienne regalia; although the exact number of sheds was not detailed.

In other areas of the cemetery, a rain cistern for collection of rooftop runoff was built, 20 feet in diameter, 18 feet deep; a large well dug and topped; a fence erected. The blacksmith's shop was moved a short distance; and a two tenement dwelling house was built near the stable for the stablekeepers.

Finally, a conservatory was built, 111 feet by 24 feet by 28 feet high, double the width of the earlier structure, directly adjoining the present greenhouses, because more room was required for the tropical plants, as previously stood in the propagating houses until readied for planting along the avenue of the main gate and other prominent places, an activity of which financial notation was made in the annual report. Increased labor costs were due in large part to the planting of ornamental beds of flowers. (4)

1874

No records are available for this year.

1875

1875 marks the changing of the Trustees' definition of the fiscal year, which now begins on February 1. Meanwhile , throughout the past twelve months, iron fences and hedges were removed from proprieters' lots just as nearly a decade before, during the Civil War; Consecration Avenue was extended to Cedar, near its junction at Forest Hills Avenue; while another avenue, 2,000 feet in length was created, extending from Nsutan, near Eliot Hills through the southwest section of the Seaverns' lot to Chestnut Avenue near Walk Hills Street. (While no name is mentioned, the avenue is most likely Palm Avenue, mentioned in 1877.)

The total land holdings of the corporation are now 226 acres compared to half that amount, 104 acres in 1856; and there is mention among architectural notes of a heretofore unspecified blacksmith's house; which may have been erected in 1874, the year for which no records are available.(6)

1876

As early as 1848 Dearborn mentioned the linking of Lake Hibiscus with another water body, Jamaica Pond, if necessary, to provide continuous fresh water flows for the fountains, watering, and to prevent stagnation of the lakes.

On June 10, 1876, Alvah Kittredge died. "He was one of three persons, who, by use of their own names, in advance of city action, secured the tract which has now grown into Forest Hills Cemetery." (The other two were probably Head, and certainly Dearborn.) Meanwhile, the rough ledge to the left of the gateway, was tamed into a green slope. Two avenues Oakland and Yew were completed in such a fashion that Oakland runs from Consecration to the lower gate lodge, while Yew runs from the main gate, uniting with Oakland at the base of Chapel Hill.

A steam pump, screened from view by evergreens, was put at Lake Hibiscus, an earthen pipe 10 inches in diameter laid so as to connect Lake Hibiscus with a lake partially dug, lying below Blue Hill Avenue, the latter of which is to be completed next year. We recall that finally a bell tower and observatory, 100 feet high, was completed atop Snow Flake Hill.(7)

1877

The report for this year states: "No striking improvements" were made. But, Palm Avenue was competed; Citron Avenue was extended and joined to Spruce, thus paralleling Walk Hill Street, and the space between Walk Hill and Citron was planted with trees and shrubs. The report continues:

"A large amount of work has been done at the Grotto. Among other improvements there, a reservoir has been built on the highest part, to supply the several fountains below, the water being forced up by the steam pump at Lake Hibiscus; the unsightly stumps have been removed and replaced by rocks. Catch basins have been constructed to hold gutter run-off." (8)

This work is close enough to Dearborn's original plan of a few decades earlier to allow us to speculate that the fountains were contained in the Lake Dell area, and in fact, as the next year's annual report and meeting minutes reveal, we would be correct in our assumption.

1878

During this year, most of the work was directed toward Consecration Avenue and the fountain, so that the Magnolia-Consecration Avenue area was greatly improved; and Cochituate water was introduced during the summer, having been carried as far as Lake Dell, in which a small fountain has been placed, thus keeping its basin filled with water. (So the lake won't again dry up, a problem of concern to Dearborn.) Another fountain was placed during the Fall, opposite the Receiving Tomb; the future plans for which area include both the addition of a rustic basin, and the creation, introduction and enhancement of a flower border.(9)

1879

No records are available for this year. (10)

SECTION IV: CHAPTER IV:
THE DECADE OF THE EIGHTEEN SEVENTIES - ENDNOTES

1. Forest Hills Cemetery, Board of Commissioners, <u>Annual Report, 1870</u>; and <u>Meeting Minutes, 1870.</u>

2. <u>Ibid., 1871</u>; Both entries.

3. <u>Ibid., 1872</u>; Both entries.

4. <u>Ibid., 1873</u>; Both entries.

5. No records obtainable for 1874.

6. Forest Hills Cemetery, Board of Commissioners, <u>Annual Report, 1875</u>; <u>Meeting Minutes, 1875.</u>

7. <u>Ibid., 1876</u>; Both entries.

8. <u>Ibid., 1877</u>; Both entries.

9. <u>Ibid., 1878</u>; Both entries.

10. No records obtainable for 1879.

Chapter V

The Decade Of The Eighties

1880 - 1883

Other than the installation of a six inch drain pipe from Lake Dell to Lake Hibiscus, to accommodate overflow occasionally generated by Lake Dell, very little activity is recorded; except for the continued removal of iron fences from the proprietor's lots; perhaps the lull before the storm of activity experienced in 1883.

The two main areas of activity for this year included the grading, sodding, and planting around Consecration Avenue, which thus yielded valuable lots on the road's north side; and the construction of a new chapel and new office building, deemed needed because the offices at the gateway now seemed "contracted". Deciding to combine the chapel and office, the Trustees asked several architects to submit plans for consideration; among which was that of Van Brundt and Howe, the one subsequently adopted; the objectification of which was accomplished by two contractors named Cressey and Noyes. The cellar excavations were begun, although work was generally slow, since workmen were forced to cut through solid ledge; still, the building was scheduled to be finished by Christmas of 1884.(1)

The following description, extrapolated from the March 17, 1884 Annual Report covering activities of the previous year, is informative and helpful.

DESCRIPTION OF THE MORTUARY CHAPEL AND SUPERINTENDENT'S OFFICE

The building containing the mortuary chapel and the Superintendent's office of the Forest Hills Cemetery, now under contract, is to be erected next northwest of the main gateway, with which it is intended to form a harmonious group. The southwest front towards the cemetery is placed on a line with the cemetery wall, the mass of the new structure projecting outside the enclosure.

.....In extreme length the building is 83 feet from southeast to northwest: its greatest width is 39 feet.

.....The superintendent's office is nearest the main gateway. In interior dimensions it is 16 x 24 feet, with a private office 8 to 10 1/2 feet, and the suite has an ample, fire-proof safe, a toilet room, chimney piece, closets, and stairs to the basement (which extends under the whole building) and to the watchman's lodgings in the roof. The office is entered by a doorway towards the grounds, and from outside the grounds by an open cloistered porch which occupies the outer side of the office building, and forms an important feature of the design as viewed by one approaching the cemetery. The windows of the office command a view of the grounds inside the enclosure, and of the approaching avenue outside. To this avenue the office building presents a gabled front, and beyond this gable rises a higher gable crowned with a bell-cote tower 60 feet high, forming the end wall of the chapel. From this wall the chapel extends northwesterly 30 feet wide and 50 feet long, finishing with a polygonal apse which is the whole width of the nave. The chapel has a wooden roof of opened timber supported by arches, trusses of ash, which spring from columns with carved capitals, giving a total interior height from the floor to apex of 35 feet. Within, the chapel walls of the nave are 15 feet high. In the upper part of these walls, on either side, is a freize of lancet windows, and the apse receives light from five larger and longer lancrets covered on the outside with gablets or canopies, breaking through the main cornice of the apse. These windows are to be filled with stained glass under the contract. The bays formed by the interior trusses are marked on the outside by buttresses. The floor of the chapel is laid in hard woods; it has a broad central aisle, with benches against the side walls capable of accommodating 92 people, with seats against the wall; and there is a paneled wainscot all around the chapel, in ash, 9 feet high. On the gable wall of the chapel, opposite the apse, is an octagonal singing gallery corbeled over from the wainscot; over this hangs a small organ, which is the principle interior feature of this end of the room. This gallery is approached by the staircase which gives access to the second story of the wing. Above the wainscot the walls are to be plastered and decorated in distemper. The rest of the interior is in wood, the roof being sheathed with stained pine and defined by molded rafter-ribs in ash.

.....The chapel has two entrances, both furnished with vestibules; one of these opens at the end of the cloister porch, by which entrance is obtained from outside the grounds. But the main approach to the chapel is within the grounds, by a large gabled *porte-corchere* spanning the driveway which skirts the southwest front of the building. Both entrances are paved with stone and have stone steps.

...The new building, like the gateway, is in Gothic form. Its walls are of Roxbury puddingstone rubble with facing of yellow free-stone, and the roofs are covered with red slate. The gables of the porte-cochere and of the bell-cote tower are adorned with crockets corresponding in character with those over the gateway to the cemetery.

1884

A letter from architects Van Brundt and Howe states that "no attempt has been made to cheapen the work at any point"; since the buildings cost $33,478.00, they were indeed not cheap for the times, but at least now, they were finished, handsomely. On the remainder of the cemetery, work progressed as usual, with catch basins and gutters being built and for perhaps the first time in several decades, the reports fail to divulge footage listings for the avenues in their annual report. There was, however, an explanation given for the removal of the iron fences from the lots(2) The Commissioners stated:

"It affords us gratification to note the removal of 18 iron enclosures which we regard as a sign that there is an increasing sentiment in favor of dispensing with enclosures which are not in harmony with the natural beauties of this sacred spot." (3)

In sentiment, this comment closely parallels Jacob Bigelow's distaste, evidenced at Mount Auburn Cemetery, for any such enclosures which he felt broke up the expanse of the landscape, hence creating a restless attitude in an area of peace. He personally felt such enclosures were a symbol of private territorialism inconsistent with the virtue of brotherhood ideally characterizing cemeteries.

1885

Of the few activities occurring in 1885 the significant ones are also sad ones: the death of Joseph Tucker, Board Secretary and Commissioner for 37 years, at the age of 85, on April 21; and the death of Superintendent, Oliver Moulton, on July 15. (4)

1886

In 1886, improvements were made, but only generally noted by Joseph Balch, author of the Annual Report, and then President of the Board; of which improvements mentioned we know that a section between Catalpa and Maple Avenues was prepared for lots, as was a section along Citron Avenue; that lots on Consecration Avenue, Magnolia and Caladium paths were finished near the Forest Avenue range; and that the Field of Manoah was scheduled for grading. Lake Hibiscus received unspecified attention. Meanwhile, beds of hardy plants were rearranged, to be planted with rhododendrons, azaleas, heath, andromedas, and lilies; and some unknown alterations were made in ornamenting Main Avenue from Morton Street, to the entrance. John Barker, formerly of Pine Grove Cemetery in Lynn, replaced Oliver Moulton as Superintendent; and amidst the annual report property notations, 4 replaces 2; although it is unclear if this number represents tenements or merely living space. (5)

1887

George Lewis, for 39 years a commissioner for Forest Hills Cemetery and later a treasurer, died. An early advocate of the cemetery, it was felt that "no officer rendered it better service than he...In all the relations of it he illustrated the attributes of good citizenship, and the graces of a true Christian manhood. We shall do well, therefore, to emulate the example he has left us." (These phrases form perhaps the nicest tribute afforded any commissioner by his associates to date, even General Dearborn.).

Other events included repaving of Forest Hills Avenue, the completion of the Field of Manoah, the planting of those hardy plants mentioned in last year's report, the repair of the tropical plant and propagating houses, construction of brick-framed hot beds for the greenhouse and a new building, 18 x 26 feet, located at the rear of the greenhouses, intended for storage on the lower floor and a workshop on the second floor.(6)

1888

In 1888, tropical plants were arranged around Lake Hibiscus forming a garden, which from all accounts was well-received. Cobblestones near the inside gate on Forest Hills Avenue were replaced by concrete; and a concrete crosswalk was removed from Union Terrace to the Chapel entrance and regarded. (7).

1889

The Commissioners split into two committees: one on the "Care of the Cemetery Grounds"; one called, the "Finance Committee". The Field of Manoah's attaining capacity necessitated the preparation of the Field of Heth on Canterbury Street as an alternative, and so it was scheduled to be ready for burials in the Spring of 1892.

SECTION IV: CHAPTER IV:
THE DECADE OF THE EIGHTEEN - EIGHTIES

1.   Forest Hills Cemetery, Board of Commissioners, <u>Annual Reports for 1880, 1881, 1882, 1883</u>; and Cemetery, <u>Meeting Minutes 1880, 1881, 1882, 1883</u>.

2.   Forest Hills Cemetery, Board of Commissioners, <u>Annual Report for 1884</u>, especially March 17, 1884 ; Cemetery, <u>Meeting Minutes 1884</u>..

3.   <u>Annual Report for 1884</u>, entry on Van Brundt and Howe; Cemetery <u>Meeting Minutes, 1884.</u>

4.   <u>Ibid.,1887</u>; Both sources

5.   <u>Ibid., 1886</u>;Both sources

6.   <u>Ibid.,1887</u>; Both sources.

7.   <u>Ibid., 1888</u>; Both sources.

8.   <u>Ibid., 1889</u>; Both sources.

CHAPTER VI

THE DECADE OF THE NINETIES

1890

Topping the expenditures list is an entry for land costing $85,450.00, by which we are alerted to the most significant events of this year as two land purchases, the estates of abutters, Milton and Peters; the acquisition of which swelled the cemeterial land coffers substantially:

> The new purchase embraces the Milton and Peters estates, enlarging the grounds to 201 1/2 acres. These two estates have frontage on Morton Street of about 2,000 feet and when the contemplated improvements are carried out, at the intersection of Forest Hills Avenue and Morton Street, which will in part correspond with the entrance to Franklin Park on the opposite side, it will very materially add to the already attractive appearance of the entrance.

Lastly, the Field of Heth will be available for use next Spring, as work has finished in this area.(1)

1891

During this year of the decade of the nineties, a bridge was built connecting the Peters and Milton estates, across the ravine opposite Magnolia Avenue (over present-day Greenwood Avenue), which was designed by W. G. Preston, with the materials taken largely from cemetery grounds, except for the Milford granite cappings. The bridge was scheduled to be 128 feet long, by 23 feet wide, with a flight of steps on the north side giving access to the avenue under the bridge, an octagon recess on the north side, with buttresses at each end of the structure, forming a graceful, slightly curved arch on both sides of the bridge, relieving the long outlines of the structure, which can easily be viewed from Forest Hills Avenue. The landscaping includes hardy trees to be planted in the Spring of 1892.

While the bridge required $14,000.00; enclosing the Milton and Peters lots equally expensive, plus an additional, 3,000.00 for a total of $17,000. In another area of the cemetery, the Morton street entrance was improved by setting back the fence from the stone cottage on Forest Hills Avenue to Morton Street allowing an avenue on both sides of a large triangle on Morton Street, undoubtedly where the present day tree-studded triangular oasis exists near the entrance to the cemetery.

As Dearborn had advocated years, in fact decades earlier, "The system of water pipes has been completed, and now extends throughout the grounds, connecting 30 hydrants" thus facilitating summer work, upkeep of nearby shrubbery and plants, and a convenience for visitors bringing flowers, and plants.(2)

1892

No new projects were considered or undertaken during this year, however, planting around the bridge and at the entrance island, along Forest Hills Avenue and Morton Street, was done, and a map of the estates drawn.

1893

Major development centered around the Milton estate, which was found to contain large quantities of ledge, later used to build a roadbed from the Forest Hills Avenue cottage to the new building; while major events focused on the Canterbury Street area. Instead of purchasing land, the Financial Committee refers to a sale of land owned by the cemetery, to the city of Boston, for $22,425.00 which was then added to the general fund. (4).

1894

Entries for this year inform us that the Superintendent's house was enlarged and improved; a new visitor's/proprietor's building begun on Beech Avenue near Canterbury Street, toward the entrance; composed of stone taken from the cemetery which will also have a tool cellar for general storage. Lake Dell was filled in to allow for the widening of different avenues leading from the front entrance to other parts of the cemetery. (5)

The Receiving Tomb was reconstructed, giving larger and better accommodations, and Lake View and Pearl Avenues were graded.(6)

Graded during the previous year, Lake View and Pearl Avenue lots were sodded: "The new Lake View section has been laid out in lots and is a very beautiful and desirable location, on high ground, commanding a fine view of Lake Hibiscus." We recall, this description borders on the ideal spirit and location for a resting place advocated by various factions of the beautification movement, for whom Edward Everett had espoused the ideal image of burial, "removed from all the discordant scenes of life", safe, beautiful, away from encroachment of unpleasant thought or deed.

Five hundred new graves were added to the Field of Heth by the trenching and loaming of a new tract of land situated along Canterbury Street; while Hackamatack Avenue, also along this area of the cemetery, was finished and planted.

Organizationally, the Board of Trustees consolidated the offices of Secretary and Treasurer. (7)

1897

Throughout the past 12 months, the avenues and paths were covered with Roxbury crushed stone; in all, 1,069 tons were purchased for this object. Meanwhile, the other expenses were for: the purchase of land adjoining the greenhouses, not the Flanders estate ($10,500.00) sewer assessments ($1,631), and the employment of watchmen to patrol the grounds at night.(8)

1898

Since this year marked the fiftieth anniversary of the operation of the cemetery, accordingly, an elaborate annual report was assembled, which consolidated the first report issued, a record of Consecration exercises, and the most recent report of operations and accomplishments. This booklet was published in February. Throughout the remaining ten months of the year, the following improvements were made: three new greenhouses and eight new cold frames were constructed; a drain was built, 2327 feet long, connecting the greenhouse furnace pits to avoid flooding; Forest Avenue was extended by 450 feet, thus completing its course from Bellevue to Hackamatack; the Field of Heth was extended by additional plots of land added at the junction of Hackamatack and Forest Avenues; grading in the Rural avenue section was completed; and a rustic wall of stone was built on the outer edge of Magnolia Avenue, "rising Consecration Hill" and relieving it of its unfinished appearance.(9)

1899

During this, the final year under consideration here, one large purchase of land was effected: 30 acres in total, the remaining portion of the Morton estate, which rounded out the corner of Canterbury and Morton Streets; and the grounds around the new greenhouses were laid out and borders planted. This is also the first year that photographs have become sufficiently popularized as to be included in the annual report. (10).

Section IV: Chapter VI:
The Decade Of The Nineties

1. Forest Hills Cemetery, Board of Commissioners' <u>Annual Report, 1890</u>; Cemetery <u>Meeting Minutes, 1890</u>; Purchase Orders.

2. Commissioners'<u> Annual Report, 1891</u>; Cemetery <u>Meeting Minutes, 1891</u>.

3. <u>Ibid</u>., 1892; Both sources.

4.. <u>Ibid</u>., 1893, Both sources.

5. <u>Ibid</u>., 1894; Both sources.

6. <u>Ibid</u>., 1895; Both sources.

7. <u>Ibid</u>., 1896; Both sources.

8. <u>Ibid</u>., 1897.

9. <u>Ibid</u>., 1898.

10. <u>Ibid</u>., 1899.

SECTION V:

APPENDIXES

LAND ACQUISITIONS - SIGNIFICANT PURCHASE ORDERS

Year	Acreage	Seller
1847	55	Seaverns and Parkinson
1852	32	Bordering Lake Hibiscus
1855		Fowler gravel mound
1859		Chandler, Canterbury Street
1864	6	Walk Hill from Warren
1862	22	From Fowler, on Walk Hill, Canterbury
1866	21	From Peters, on Forest Hills Avenue
1867		Two purchases from I. Carey, Forest Hills Avenue area
1867		From H. D. Williams, near Forest Hills Avenue
1868		From Simons, Gravel pile on Bourne Street
1870	19	From Seaverns, on the north line of the cemetery
1871	37	From heirs of Betsey Williams; Canterbury Street, south side
1897		From Flanders
1899	30	From Morton, at Canterbury Street and Morton, corner

Chronological Synopsis

Day	Year	Activity
October 5	1846	Mayor John Clarke's address
November	1846	Joint Special Committee
March	1847	Joint Special Committee passes the buck
April	1847	New City Council formed with Dearborn as Mayor
Summer	1847	New City Council buys first located land (Dearborn and two others)
September	1847	Dearborn submits his report; Seaverns' land obtained, but not Warren's
November 9	1847	Seaverns' Purchase Order
-	1847	Parkinson's Purchase Order
March	1848	Commissioners chosen
April 25	1848	Work begun
June	1848	Consecrated
July	1848	Named "Forest Hills Cemetery"
-	1851	Dearborn dies.
-	1857	Skeletons found on Consecration Hill
-	1868	Cemetery incorporated
-	1898	Fiftieth Anniversary Celebration

CEMETERY ACTIVITY ORGANIZED BY STRUCTURE, YEAR, AND EVENT

Area:	Year	Activity
Barn	1853	Barn and shed moved from Seaverns' land to central location
	1862	Barn placed on Fowler land; shed added to barn
Beech Avenue	1894	Built:: Visitors' Lodge plus Storage Cellar
Blacksmith's Shop	1854	Erected near Canterbury Street, south corner of cemetery
	1869	Moved from cemetery land to opposite Canterbury Street
	1873	Moved again.
Bridge	1891	Built: by W. G. Preston of cemetery rock and Milton granite
Chandler House	1860	Renovated
Chapel	1883	Begun; architects were Van Brundt and Howe
	1884	Finished (Gothic; of Roxbury Puddingstone; rubble with yellow free-stone facings)
Cottage	1848	Superintendent's office, built near main gate.
	1866	Superintendent's office , moved to Carey land.
	1868	Enlarged by one room
	1868	Double tenement built for Assistant Superintendent

Field of Ephron	1856	Started, single graves (replaced MacPhelah)
	1857	Fence built around it; Chapel Avenue built nearby
	1864	Filled in August; new site sought
Field of MacPhelah	1850	Begun along south side of cemetery (single graves)
Field of Manoah	1864	Started in southern end (single graves)
Field of Heth	1890	Begun
	1892	Finished
	1896	Extended
	1898	Extended by 700 graves

CEMETERY ACTIVITY ORGANIZED BY STRUCTURE, YEAR, AND EVENT

Area	Year	Activity
Peripheral Fences	1848	Rustic wooden fences erected
	1868	Iron fence erected
Lot Fences/ Enclosures	1848	First one erected; hedges follow in three years
	1864	First one removed from lot
Forest Hills Avenue	1853	Graded
	1865	Trees removed to facilitate main entrance view
	1866	Two purchases: Peters and Carey
	1867	Three purchases: H. D. Williams; 2 of Carey
	1887	Paved
	1892	Island at Morton Street laid out; not yet planted.
Fountains	1877	One place in Lake Dell
	1877	One placed opposite the receiving tomb
Gates		
Main	1807	Chosen, along Walk Hill Street, south side of cemetery; along Warren's land

	1848	Replotted along Parkinson's land; northerly side of cemetery
Dearborn's (Egyptian)	1848, June	Dearborn's Egyptian gateway approved; of wood, modeled after Garnsey on the Nile.
	1848-1850	Dearborn's Main Gateway with flanking lodges built..
	1850	Trees laid out.
Panter's (Gothic)	1863	Plans for Gothic gateway designed by Charles Panter of Boston approved.
	1864	Actual work begun on Panter's Gothic Gate
	1865	Stones laid and copper box, cornerstone, inserted underneath
	1876	Rough ledge at left gate fixed; graded for green lawn
	1888	Cobblestone, inside, near gate removed; paved with concrete.

CEMETERY ACTIVITY ORGANIZED BY STRUCTURE, YEAR, AND EVENT

Area	Year	Activity
Greenhouse	1860	Finished.
	1865	$300.00 of flowers sold
	1868	Relocated from central part of cemetery to near main gate, enlarged, renamed: the Conservatory. 3 new propagating houses built.
	1873	New Conservatory; adjoining greenhouses built..
	1887	New building, 18 x 36, storage area built
	1898	Three new greenhouses built.
Hackamatack Avenue	1897	Begun.
	1898	Extended between Forest and Bellevue
Lakes, Dell	1864	First mention
	1881	Connected by 6-inch diameter pipe to Lake Hibiscus; per Dearborn's plan of years earlier.
	1894	Filled in.
Hibiscus	1853	Enlarged; Spring Island formed

	1854	Enlarged, Swan Island formed; encircling wall built.
	1855	Surface area of lake enlarged
	1856	Wooden fence erected on South side, to avoid visitor accidents
	1859	Drain built
	1877	Pipe run from Lake Hibiscus to reservoir leading to fountains
	1876	Steam pump laid and 10-inch pipe laid to Blue Hill Avenue Reservoir.
Mount Warren	1864	Wall erected
Nursery	1848	Located in central part of cemetery
	1850	Active planting of trees (imported, oriental)
	1855	Moved from central to south side of cemetery
Office	1848	Built on Fountain Hill, sundial outside, bronze plaque on boulder
	1883	New office combining chapel to replace old office; now near main gateway; Gothic, puddingstone, faced with yellow freestone; red slate roof; 1/2 size of present office.
Office, cont.	1884	Finished

Observatory Tower	1848	Rustic observatory built around oak tree on summit of Consecration Hill, 25 feet high, affording views of Blue Hills, Jamaica Plain, Brighton, Dorchester Bay.
	1876	New Bell Tower; replaces Observatory; on Snow-Flake Hill.
Omnibus	1852	Started to shuttle visitors around cemetery especially to a favorite attraction: Lake Hibiscus
Stable	1869	Built near Superintendent's Cottage
	1873	New stable built on Canterbury
Soldier's Lot	1862	Prepared
	1864	Foundation laid; completion of encircling granite fence.
Swan Building	1872	Built; visitors lodge for swans and birds only, 28 x 12.
Underground Water	1892	System of 30 interconnected hydrants serving areas all around the cemetery: completed.

BIBLIOGRAPHY

Bigelow, Jacob. A History of Mount Auburn: Its Scenes, Its Beauties, and Its Lessons. Boston: James Monroe and Co., 1861.

Branch Alliance of all Souls Unitarian Church, The Roxbury Magazine, Boston: George Ellis, 1899.

Crafts, Augustus William. Forest Hills Cemetery: Its Establishment, Progress, Scenery, Monuments, etc. Roxbury: John backup, 1855.

Dearborn, Nathaniel. Guide to Mount Auburn. James Monroe and Company, Boston, 1861.

Ellis, Charles M. The History of Roxbury Town. Samuel G. Drake, Boston, 1847.

Fein, Albert. Frederick Law Olmstead and the American Environmental Tradition. George Brasilia, New York, 1972.

"The American City: The Ideal and the Real", in Edgar Kaufmann, The Rise of American Architecture, Metropolitan Museum and Praegar Publishers, New York, 1970.

Flagg, Wilson. Mount Auburn: Its Scenes, Its Beauties and It Lessons. James Monroe and Company, Boston 1861

Forest Hills Cemetery. Annual Reports, 1849-1900.

Beautiful and Historic Forest Hills Cemetery, pamphlet available at the cemetery, unknown publisher.

Meeting Minutes (of the Commissioners/Trustees); 1846-1900.

Catalogue of the Proprietors of Forest Hills Cemetery. Rockwell and Churchill Press, Boston: 1900. Also available for 1892.

Foxcroft, Frank. Mount Auburn. (other information unavailable).

Harris, Neil. The Artist in American Society: The Formative Years, 1790-1860, George Brazillier, New York, 1966.

Hecksher, August, Open Spaces: The Life of American Cities, Harper and Rose, New York, 1977.

Kelleher, Diane; also Kelleher-Breen, Diane. Forest Hills Cemetery: FHC:KRN, Research, lecture notes, text, appendixes, photographs, maps, 1979.

Kull, Andrew. New England Cemeteries: A Collector's Guide. Stephen Greene Press, Vermont.

Marion, John Francis. Famous and Curious Cemeteries. Crown Publishers, New York, 1977.

Roxbury Municipal Government City Documents (Municipal Registers, Mayoral Addresses, and Committee Reports), located at Boston Public Library, Municipal Records Department.

Watts, Francis O.: Fearing , Albert: and Wilkins, John, "An Address to the Citizens of Boston and Vicinity on the Subject of a Rural Cemetery". Eastburn's Press, Boston, 1850.

Whitehill, Walter Muir. <u>Architecture Boston: The Boston Society of Architects</u>. Barre Publishing, Massachusetts.

About the Author

Born and educated in Massachusetts, at age sixteen Ms. Kelleher began her undergraduate studies in the Liberal Arts at prestigious Wheaton College in Norton. By twenty, she had received the degree of "Bachelor of Arts with Distinction" from Simmons College, Boston. Graduating in the top five percent of her class, while majoring in Sociology, Economics and Art History, beyond "Distinction" additional baccalaureate honors conferred included: Academy (Collegiate Honor Society), Departmental Recognition (History of Art), Dean's List and receipt of academic grants.

Further general art historical studies and specialized new directions reflecting a burgeoning interest in American Art and Culture, as well as European Painting of the Nineteenth Century, were undertaken within the Department of the History of Art, Master of Arts and Doctor of Philosophy program at Boston University's Graduate School of Arts and Sciences. By age twenty-four she had independently researched and authored her first book and the first art historical book ever written on Boston artist, Lilian Westcott Hale. Unlikely Icon was independently researched and written a year later.

An independent research author in the arts, her documentary books include:

<u>Enchantment: The Art and Life of Lilian Westcott Hale, America's Linear Impressionist</u>;

<u>Marvelous Miniatures and Perfect Pastels: The Art and Life of Laura Coombs Hills, America's Lyric Impressionst.</u>

Fictional works include:

<u>The Fantasmagorical Feline Adventures of Little Miss Libby and the Mystery of the Rare, Turquoise Blue, Boston Trumpeter Swan</u>;

and

<u>The Secrets of Willow Creek</u>.

www.ingramcontent.com/pod-product-compliance
Lightning Source LLC
Chambersburg PA
CBHW061303280526
45784CB00002B/870